HAVE A BEAUTY DAY

One Woman's Winding Path to Healing Generational Trauma

Catherine Wright

Just Wright Publishers
Duluth, Minnesota

Copyright © 2023
Just Wright Publishers
Duluth, Minnesota 55803-1605
All rights reserved.
Printed in the United States of America

Author photograph: Adeline Wright
Cover design: Mike Smíšek

∞

Wright, Catherine 1957-
Have a Beauty Day: One Woman's Winding Path to Healing Generational
   Trauma / Catherine Wright; edited by Mara Hart and Meredith Cornett.
   Includes bibliographical references.
   ISBN 979-8-218-13528-7 (paperback)
      1. Wright, Catherine M. 1957-. 2. Two Harbors, Minnesota. 3. Knife River,
Minnesota. 4. Owatonna, Minnesota. 5. Minnesota State Public School. 6.
Minnesota State Board of Control. 7. Willmar State Asylum. 8. Yvonne Prettner
Solon. 9. Elisabeth Mannering Congdon. 10. Minnesota History Center.

*To Adeline, Gala,
and future generations of emotional warriors*

Contents

	Editors' Note by Mara Hart and Meredith Cornett	7
1.	Motherless Child	9
2.	My Search: The Knife River	35
3.	The Orphanage	47
4.	New Name, New Life	59
5.	My Life Growing Up	99
6.	Betty's Decline and Death	125
7.	My Search: The Records	145
8.	Closing Thoughts	163
	Acknowledgements	173
	Interview with the Author	175
	Appendices: Selection of Original Historical Documents	179
	About the Author	212

Editors' Note

Cathy spent more than 15 years writing this book—persisting in her work even as she began to experience symptoms associated with frontotemporal degeneration (behavioral variant), a rare form of early onset dementia. The manuscript was in more than one hundred different files in a format that was not editable on Mara's 2012 MacBook. It took many people and many days to copy and reformat the files in order to get them into an editable form.

We have made no attempt to revise or to alter Cathy's story, as written by her. Mara puzzled out a logical order for the complete manuscript and made necessary corrections for spelling and punctuation. Meredith stitched together the edited files from Mara, formatted them, and organized the manuscript and supplemental materials for publication. Our goal was to stay true to Cathy's voice, while also providing flow and context that would be helpful to readers.

Please give grace for whatever inconsistencies and complications you encounter. This is Cathy's story, based on her lived experience through the lens of fluctuating cognitive capacity. We believe this fluctuating perspective is as valuable as the narrative itself. We hope Cathy's work will enhance your understanding of trauma and its inherited effects.

Cathy's writing of this book was a labor of love for herself and future generations of her family. It was our love of Cathy that inspired us to collaborate on editing and publishing *Have a Beauty Day*.

Mara Hart and Meredith Cornett
January 2023

Part 1
Motherless Child

I

June 1925, Mary Norgren

"Mama!"

"Yes, Florence?"

"Where are you going with baby Betty?"

"To the river, dear. Would you like to come along?"

"Yes, Mama. Why do you have baby Betty in the basket, Mama?"

"The Lord has told me to put her in a basket, dear. The Lord gives me instructions and I must follow them, Florence, or he will be very angry and cause bad things to happen." Mary Norgren looks down at the six-year-old who is asking her all these questions. "I must do what God asks, Florence, just as you are to do what Mama asks of you." Mary raises her brow as she looks for the response from her daughter. Florence's upraised eyes look deeply into her Mama's, as she smiles to appease and nods with more trepidation than a six–year-old girl should have. "Come along, little one, and we will do God's work together." And they move down the hill's footpath to the Knife River.

TWO MEN ARE fly fishing near the railroad trestle, just over a quarter of a mile up from the mouth of the Knife River: "Perfect day for this," one says. The other loudly whispers, just above the sound of the river's gentle flow.

"I can feel a big one coming upstream right now, right to …" He pauses and his friend looks up thinking a fish is on the line. "The Basket! The BASKET!" he hollers to his friend standing to the left and downstream, as he starts running downstream after a floating basket that is heading toward the big lake. "Grab it, man! "You've got to get it! There is something alive in there!" he shouts with urgency. The other man moves quickly over the rocky bottom, through the water, determined to stop the basket from going out into the lake. Just in time, he grabs it.

"You got it? You ok?" the other man hollers as he waddles toward his friend who is working to hold his fishing rod and the newly attained basket and not lose his balance on the rocky, unstable riverbed.

"Here, give me your rod," he says, taking it from his friend as they gently touch the small dirty towel that is moving dramatically from whatever is underneath it. One peek and in unison they gasp. "What in God's name?" Carefully moving toward the shore and up onto the river's edge where they started from, they pull aside the towel. The man carrying the basket gasps as he sees a beautiful, dark-haired baby, blinking to get used to the daylight again and looking up at him. The other man shakes his head in disbelief.

Both men are looking from the basket to upstream and then back to the basket, trying to figure out where it came from. "What in God's name is going on? It's a terrible thing, a terrible thing," one repeats, reaching in as the tiny little human watches without making a sound, arms and feet moving and jumping. The man reaches in to feel the limbs and the trunk for signs of trauma or deformity. "This baby seems fine," he states with conviction, and adds, "What are we going to do now?"

"We're taking this basket up to town and finding out what the hell is going on," his friend replies. "What a thing to find floating toward the big lake." shaking his head from side to side, "What a thing to find, poor little thing."

"Floating right out into the big lake," the older man says, shaking his head from side to side, "What if we weren't here? Ah, I hate to think of it!"

One holds the basket while the other gathers their gear and belongings and they head to Two Harbors to the police station.

(Editorial note: There are some inconsistencies at this point. We believe that the baby in the basket may have been Baby Betty May, who "did not survive." See Section III, p. 16).

II

January 1974, Betty Wright

Somewhere inside there lies a shame.
    A shame that takes hold and won't let go.
    Others knowing about it terrifies me, though I speak of it out loud as matter of fact, the depth of it, the truth of the evil that it holds must be kept hidden.
    If it is ever fully revealed, they may lock me away in the insane asylum, like they did my mother, and her sister. Please, help me keep these secrets. Most importantly, keep them from me. If I unlock the whole story, it may destroy me. It is in me, like the devil. It lurks and sneaks out when I least want it to. It is referred to as "the crazies."
    I married my childhood sweetheart, a brilliant, loving, angry, violent, and alcoholic man, and have given birth to six children, five of whom are alive. At age forty-eight, I am being hospitalized for a nervous breakdown.

III

From what I heard from my mother, Betty Lois Wright, I pictured what happened in the yellow house near the Historical Marker at the Knife River, Minnesota rest area. I have wondered and thought about this my entire life.

May 1922, Mary Norgren

"This house is too damn small!" Mary Norgren cries, pregnant and exhausted. The house is messy with dishes undone and Mary unkempt, as are her children. Her husband's rage about how little gets done while he's away started all this.

"I wish you wouldn't keep having babies," he says, looking up for a moment and then back to the floor, as he sits at the small kitchen table.

"I wish that more than you do," she says, with such sadness. "I wish it more than you!" she repeats, her voice turning into a rage-filled shout. A dirty, wet dishrag comes flying out of her hand, landing on the floor a few inches from where baby Dougal sits, just two years old and watching the fight begin. He holds a ragged little blanket and sucks on his fist, rocking forward and back. The longing to be near his father is all that he feels. He had watched the rag coming towards him and land, and felt no need to move, until his papa stood up. The energy changed, and Dougal James knew to crawl away and find a safe place to hide. His nine-year-old brother, Deward, is out, running around the woods in the small logging town named after the river that it's nestled around, Knife River. He doesn't stick around much when his pa is home.

Eight-year-old Vernon likes to run with Deward, when he'll allow it. Today he was fine with it, though he did suggest that Vernon stay home and keep the other kids from getting into trouble. It was too much for Vernon to bear today, so off they ran to be boys instead of the soldiers of family war crimes. Their freedom, though, was not at all pure.

JOHN WENDELL, WHO is called "Little John," at age six, is left to defend the family. The next youngest is Doris. She is five and wants nothing to do with her papa. She has been hiding in the attic, which has been made into a bedroom with four twin mattresses strewn about, and one small dresser. The narrow and low-ceilinged stairway to get up here can be tricky for Papa when he is drunk, so in hopes of being left alone by her father, she finds her way to the farthest mattress from the door and cuddles her sweet little self up, pulling the covers over her head but not her face. Her baby sister, Florence, who is four years old, has cautiously climbed the same stairway to find a safe spot to wait out the storm. When she sees Doris she climbs in to share her safe haven.

Six-year-old Little John frantically looks for two-year-old Dougal James behind the couch, then behind the rocking chair and finally finds him under the narrow stairs backed into the furthest darkest corner, with his blanket and fist ready to soothe. "Not a bad idea," John whispers as he sneaks quietly back to the couch to a grab a blanket while shouts and punches and cries for mercy start to fly in the kitchen. Diving in under the stairs he covers himself and Dougal with the dark blanket, keeping a breathing hole open near the wall. Then he starts to wonder if they are too easily seen. He quickly decides that being outside might be the best place for them and on his hands and knees, backs himself and Dougal along the floor to make a dash outdoors. Then he bumps into something with his bottom and stops dead.

"What are you up to, little John?" his father asks. The tone is not angry but chilling, nonetheless. John does not look up, but murmurs that he is trying to get his little brother out from under the stairs and get him ready for his nap. "Hurry up," is all that is said and that gets a very quick response from Little John. He pulls Dougal out, and lifts him up as best he can, along with the small blanket, leaving the other blanket behind. He barely makes it up the stairs without the baby slipping down through his arms. He can feel his father watching him all the while. Putting baby Dougal down, he closes the attic door without looking.

The small but heavy dresser, with felt pads on each foot, that sits near the door, will not be pushed, by all who seek shelter in the attic, until the fighting starts again, so as to cover the sound of its moving.

MEANWHILE BACK IN the kitchen, the quarrel continues:

"If you don't buy me a bigger house in town and get me some help John" her voice fades off. "I can't survive this. I can't do all this alone, please believe me, I'm going insane" She begs as she cries. "We need money for food." Turning quickly to look at her angered husband, she states slowly and carefully, "If you hurt me and these kids again…" and her voice wanders off to a low mumble. A few moments of silence go by. "You give me nothing but more damn kids," she mumbles as she turns back to the kitchen sink.

Two days later Betty May is born. She did not survive.

IV

July 1927, Betty Lois

I was born in the house that sat up on a ridge, near the mouth of the Knife River, almost three years before the Great Depression. My mother, Mary, had already given birth to eight but had seven living children, ages two to fourteen. My father was a womanizing drunk, only around long enough to get Mama pregnant, again and again, against her will.

One day my mother walked the younger six of us down to the river. Deward and Vernon had run off to be teenage boys. At the swollen river's edge, Mama took the hands of two of her children and walked slowly into the water, paying no attention to how deep it was getting for my brother and sister. Dougal was seven years old but thin and not as strong and healthy as he could have been, and Albert was a scrawny four-year-old. She wasn't looking at them but staring straight ahead as the water quickly went over Albert's head. Dougal was pulling away from her, but all at once, they were joined by John, Doris and Florence. They all started to struggle in the river's forceful current, Ma's grip on their hands pulling them under. For a short time they were unable to get Dougal's and Albert's heads above the water as they screamed for Ma to stop, to let them up. Those that were older and strong enough ran into the moving waters to try to stop their mother from drowning their siblings. Water was splashing, children were pulling and tugging. I knew only to stand on the shore and cry, the fear and confusion were solid in my throat. I was only two and a half years old.

Suddenly I watched a large man with the strongest of arms pulling the drenched and lifeless children away from Ma and to the river's edge. He placed them on the ground. My brother sat upright, my sister did not. She was put on her stomach and pushed on by this man until she spit up water and coughed. My other sister came to take my hand and stand by me as we watched. She was wet and crying too. "No more of this," I could hear Ma saying. "Away you go," as she looked downstream, her arms waving and pushing it from her. She sat facing the river, half in and half out, along the edge, never once paying any attention to the life-saving efforts of the woodsman or the baffled children gathering near, as the man motioned them toward him and away from her.

My oldest brother, Deward, stood next to the woodsman as he spoke. "Is this all of you?" the woodsman asked. "Are you all accounted for?" His voice was urgent yet calm as he kept an eye on my mother who was just a few feet away from the rest of us. I watched Deward's eyes as he nodded yes, those piercing light blue eyes. When I could see most of the blue of his eyes, he was safe to be around. He was fourteen.

He protected and punished us, "the youngins," as he called us, flipping moods and actions ever so quickly and easily. Right this moment he seemed lost and unsure, his eyes were unreadable to me and I felt uneasy. I knew only that it was, once again, life or death important to stay ready to flee.

Vernon was the second oldest. His eyes were not telling like Deward's. Vernon used words to let us know how he felt.

John Wendell, gentle John as my mother used to call him, started to cry. I could feel all of our sadness flowing from him, our fear and anguish pulling on and contorting his otherwise kind and beautiful face. He was my favorite storyteller, funny and kind to me. My tears streamed as his mouth curled and frowned. He had been staring at Doris, before darting down to sit next to her, as she sat stunned and shaking, next to Flossy and me. Flossy, still holding my hand too tightly, wrapped her other hand around the shoulder of the sister who was nearly drowned. I tried to pull my strangled hand away. Flossy looked at me angrily, then softened her look and her grip, letting go to hold onto John and Doris as she told me to stay close.

The woodsman slowly moved toward her but from the side. Her head moved so slowly to look up at him but once she realized how close he was she started to holler, "Get away!" The woodsman pointed to Vernon.

"Run as fast as you can to a neighbor with a telephone. Do you know anyone nearby?" Vernon looked at Deward.

"Hargan's have a tele. Go!" Deward barked. The woodsman spoke directly to Vernon, whose eyes were not moving from the big man's face.

"Have them call the hospital. Your mother needs medical attention as do these two," his big hand shaking a pointed finger toward Doris and Albert. Albert, the youngest boy, just five and half, had come up coughing and choking but never lost consciousness like Doris had. Moving his commanding finger toward ten-year-old John Wendell the woodsman added, "You go with him, and make sure they know to get here as quickly as possible. Tell whoever is home to come and help as soon as they've made that call."

I watched my brothers run off as instructed. The woodsman put the six of us in a tight group as the sounds of the river and Mama mumbling were collecting in my head. He kept looking back at Mama, as she sat like a rock on shore facing away from us, the water flowing around her feet and her bottom. The woodsman motioned for us to stay quietly where we were. I could feel every step he took toward her in my head, like a pounding. It was as though all other sounds had disappeared.

The woodsman slowly moved toward her but from the side. Her head moved slowly to look up at him, but once she swung at him with both fists flying in circles toward his face. We winced in unison and watched as his large hand caught hers before she got anywhere with her attack. But he was gentle, his soft low mumblings were all I could hear and relief overcame me as he calmed her. She stood calmly as he walked her to a rock, sat her down and spoke to her, her hands folding and moving into her chest and neck, her eyes never moving from his. He sat down on the rock next to her, both facing us. I felt the huddle pull me in closer, as Flossy whispered, "Maybe he can help Mama." The woodsman signaled us to sit, his hand moving to his lips with one finger showing his wish for us to be quiet. We found a safe dry place, moving the huddle of us carefully and quietly, still so full of fear and sadness.

It felt like a very long time before we heard sounds from the path through the trees. Voices, brush moving, and out they came, Vernon, then John Wendell, followed by Mr. Hargan, with his wife close behind, a Bible under her arm. Mrs. Hargan had a way with Mama too, at times able to "calm the crazies," as she used to say. She would sit with her and talk about God and the devil, Jesus and sin and how we were all watched over and loved and could be saved if we believed. At home, I became filled with hope when I heard all that, and so sad and angry that neither God nor Jesus ever showed up when "the crazies" took Mama over while she hurt us. She'd say over and over, my mama, that the devil was in every one of her children. No one, but the neighbors from time to time, came to help when Papa would come home and hurt us too.

The adults huddled. The children huddled watching them.

A voice crackled over the dull murmurs. "Why are the coppers here?" Deward cried, "Who called the cops?" as he stood and then darted in small circles. Mr. Hargan came toward Deward with his hands outstretched trying to calm.

"They always come when the ambulance is called, son. They are not here to hurt you, you have my word," he said as he put his gentle hands on Deward's shoulders.

"They're not puttin' us in jail!" Deward yelled as he tried to pull away, his words full of fear, his face red and angry.

"They're not here to get you, son." Deward started moving toward the woods. We all just sat and watched too stunned and confused to move. Our attention turned to the big man coming down the footpath from the house, followed by a smaller man dressed in the same kind of clothes.

"Bill," Mr. Hargan said, moving toward him to shake his hand. The woodsman started over to them, shaking hands and exchanging names. I heard Mr. Hargan say, "This is Chief of Police Bill Hill." The big man named Bill took a long look at the huddled batch of us. "Bill, this man saved the lives of these children today. Came running out of the woods at the sound of screaming and…" Then the warm wind blew so hard I couldn't hear the rest of their words.

The rustling came again from the woods and out came two men dressed in white followed by a dark-suited man with a black bag. Everything felt like a locomotive, moving too quickly, now. The last three moved right over to Mama. The two men in white stood on either side of her as the dark-suited man stood in front of her. I watched her look at them all. I heard her start hollering, "Oh no, not me you bastards. You're not taking me, you sons of bitches." Suddenly all the adults were around her, I couldn't see Mama anymore. After a few minutes, they started to move away from each other and there was Mama in a long white shirt, with her head hanging down, held on each side by the men dressed in white, walking her slowly toward the path. Mr. Hagen was getting us all up and standing as he told us to follow Officer Hill and Mrs. Hargan, who were following a bit behind Mama and the men in white. The woodsman came to follow behind us. Eight scared and curious children who never uttered a sound and had no idea what was about to happen.

They took my mother away in a brown car.

V

On a saddened note: I found a Recorded Death of Baby Norgren, Male.

Death Date: 12 Jan 1927
Death place: Fergus Falls, Otter Tail, Minnesota
Father's name: John O. Norgren
Mother's name: Mary McNeill

Mary was committed to the Fergus Falls State Hospital in September of 1926. I think she must have been pregnant when she tried to drown the devil out of her children in the Knife River.

VI

Exactly what happened after the river incident is a pretty big unknown. It was said that John Otto moved himself and the children into the small ore-docks shipping town of Two Harbors, ten miles further up the North Shore of Lake Superior. I'm wondering if it wasn't court ordered, so many eyes could be on the family and the kids would get some help from neighbors, which it seems they did.

They would also be close to the schools and monitored there. If that plan was put into place, I suspect that Chief of Police, Bill Hill, was heading it up.

I know that my grandfather, John Otto Norgren, did not come around to becoming a good and loving father after his wife was institutionalized. Mrs. John Sandwick comes up often regarding the children and was listed as a housekeeper. I'm thinking she was not a live-in, as the documents list her husband, but I can't be sure. The older children may have been home alone after she left for the day. There is really no way to determine what her work schedule was or how she was paid. I can't imagine that John Otto became any more reliable with his paycheck, unless there were some interventions in place, official or unofficial.

This story was, like all the rest, vaguely told by my mother Betty and verified as true by other aunts, uncles and cousins, though details vary among them. They were all so young when things happened.

Betty's words, as I remember them: "My mom put me in a basket and floated me down the Knife River. Two fishermen found me and pulled me out just before I reached Lake Superior." I have not sought a police report on this incident, warned by the Two Harbors clerks that it would take too many hours for them to look for it and it may be buried so deep they might not ever find it.

She told it.

I absorbed it.

It is mine to share.

VII

April 1930, Betty Lois

I was being tapped on the belly by Albert. "Betty, come on," he said. My five-year-old eyes snap open. "Come see our breakfast!" he exclaimed with delight, as he pulled on my hand until I sat up. "Hurry up, I'm hungry" he hollered back as he ran out of the room without me. I slid my little feet over to the floor and stood up and off the mattress I shared with my sisters and shuffled myself to the doorway. The smells of fresh pancakes and crispy bacon grabbed my attention as it hurried me to quicken my descent of the stairway, scooting on my bottom, like I always did in the morning. As I reached the stair that I could look down into the dining room from, I saw a crowd. My eyes moved left and right with growing delight, to see that the company and all my sisters and brothers were already eating. Mrs. Sandwick pointed at me to come over to her. I stood to hold the railing as I hurried down and climbed up onto the chair next to her, my eyes riveted on this most wonderful table full of food. We usually didn't have this kind of breakfast other than at church.

It was full of eggs and toast, jams and sausages, pancakes and syrup. Milk in every glass in front of every child. I thought we must be having a party and that something good must have happened. Mrs. S., as I called her, put a plate down in front of me filled with pancakes, eggs and sausages. My little hands grabbed and tasted and tasted and grabbed for more, nearly forgetting to use my fork. Mrs. S. quickly, but ever so gently, reminded me. I was five and half years old and told I was very small for my age. I looked at my sister Flossy with wide eyes, only to see her smiling, wide-eyed face beaming back at me as she ate.

Feeling how soft and delicious the pancakes were in my mouth, smothered with sweet salty butter and delightful red raspberry jam, I started looking around the room, hearing the soft voices of my brothers and sisters at the table, and realizing they were all home, even my two older brothers. Then I started to notice the adult people in our house. Women that I had seen at the church and a policeman in his uniform, standing by the window watching us eat. He was a big man with big hands and a long broad face. He leaned against the frame of the opening to the dining room, arms crossed, watching us as we ate but he never said a word. He smiled at me.

Once we were all as full in our bellies as we could be, we were told to gather in the living room on the couch. Flossy took my hand as I jumped down from the chair and we walked together to sit on the floor in front of John Wendell who was on the couch next to Vernon. On the other side of Vernon was Albert, then Dougal James. Doris sat on the arm of the couch with her arm swung over the back and Deward sat on the other arm. Eight of us, waiting to be told something wonderful, as the breakfast had been so delightful. At least I assumed it was going to be good news. But the room did not feel joyful. I wanted it to be good, so my hopeful little heart kept a warm feeling inside as I sat with pleasure, surrounded by my family, assuming Papa was at work.

Mrs. S. pulled the rocking chair closer and sat down in front of us. She was no longer smiling like she was during breakfast. "I've got some pretty tough news for you kids," she said. Shaking her head and looking at Deward, then Vernon and John.

"Now what?" Deward disgustedly asked. He was the oldest and the most serious.

"Honey, your father was hit by a car last night." I didn't understand what that meant. The bodies near me started to move.

Everything started to change very quickly. Vernon stood up so quickly that it caused a push, sending Flossy and me right over.

"Is he dead?" Vernon asked. Before he finished Deward was asking the same question. My head stretched up and back to watch as they looked at each other then back to Mrs. S. "Is he?" Vernon shouted.

"Yes!" Mrs. S. stood shouting back. Then softening, said again: "Yes, yes he is."

My brothers sat back down, and I watched their eyes for a sign of how I should feel, what it meant. I looked at Flossy and she was still and emotionless, staring at Mrs. S. I could find no clues about what was happening on the faces of my sisters or brothers. Dead. "What happened to him? Where is he now?" Vernon demanded to know. He was agitated and angry. The big man spoke.

"His body is in the morgue at the hospital, son. He was taken there last night after the accident and where he died shortly after."

"I wanna see for myself," Deward said sharply, looking directly at the policeman.

The big man tilted his head sideways toward the door and started walking. Deward looked at Vernon and made the same motion with his head. Vernon shook his head, no. Deward looked at John Wendell. John looked at Mrs. S. and she shook her head "no" and said, "You go." He followed the big man out the front door.

"Why does he want to see?" Florence asked, as we watched the door.

"To be sure he is really gone," Doris answered with a pain in her voice I could understand. Stunned, we waited.

CAR KILLS TWO HARBORS RAILROAD WORKER ON ROAD
April 23, 1930

J. O. Nordgren [sic], crane operator for the D., M. & N. railroad company in the yards at Two Harbors was instantly killed at 8:30 p.m. today on state highway No. 1, one-half mile west of Two Harbors, when he stepped into the path of a passing automobile, driven by Ingwald Sandea, machinist helper in the local shops, who was on his way home on the Stanley Rd. According to his report he saw the man walking off the highway on the side of the road and just as he got to him the man stepped into the path of the car. Sandea swung out but the fender of his car struck the man throwing him into the air and through the glass of the car door. Nordgren is survived by six children; his wife is in the state hospital at Fergus Falls. Sandea, after being questioned by police, was not held, but will appear at the coroner's inquest tomorrow morning. (Appendix A)

VIII

We had no idea how much our lives were about to change, and it all happened so suddenly.

I cried, begging to take the sock doll my mom had made for me, but I was told it would be put on my bed to wait for my return. This of course made me think it would be a short trip, to the orphanage and back. I sat crying, nearly on my sister Flossy's lap, who was pushed up against the door in the front seat of the big green county car we would be traveling in for the next twelve hours. Flossy was crying too. Dougal James, Albert and Doris were all piled in the back seat, sobbing and scared, as we drove away listening to the sound of the motor and of our older brothers yelling and waving while they wailed and cried.

It was a dark and cool morning when we started out for the State Home. That is what they called it, the people that gathered us and sent us away. The older three boys were going to stay here with our Grandma Betty for the time being and would be able to write to us. I fell asleep not too long after we got on the road heading south. When I woke, Flossy was asleep with her head on the door armrest. Her hand was holding my left hand and it took me a try or two to free myself. She sure did like to hold my hand these days, I thought. I turned my head slowly to look at who was driving. I couldn't remember where I was or why.

It was just getting light outside and the woman's face that looked down at me was strange. She smiled and put one finger up to her lips to let me know not to make any noise. Then I remembered the beginning of the trip and put my head down to cry as quietly as I could. I wanted to look in the back seat to make sure Albert was still with me, and Dougal and Doris. I wanted to stand up and look back and before I knew it I was. They were all sleeping at different angles on that big back seat. Heads on hips and arms on legs. I looked at the driver and sat back down as Flossy woke a bit and held me to her while she blinked her sweet eyes at me.

It was many hours before we were allowed to stop and use the restroom in a gas station. The driver lady said we were in Hinckley. Nine long hours later, the gloomy day had come and gone and we were tired of seeing the fields of corn and rows of potatoes and farm after farm. We saw long and smoky freight trains with cars of every color and shape.

Miss Nellie was tired of driving and we were still almost an hour away from the State School. At one point, she let it slip that we were heading to an orphanage. My sister Doris was demanding to know what that meant. She just talked around that and carried on with some other story about the area we were in and the names of the cities and towns along the way. My brothers and sisters were reading each road sign out loud, asking what it meant and where we were. This road sign read OWATONNA, no one knew how to pronounce it. Miss Nellie got quiet, not helping with the name of the town. After a few minutes, the car slowed as the right blinker started to make its cootah cootah sound. I liked the sound of the turn signals. We knew we were near, the road we turned into was narrower and the sign, read out loud by the back seaters: "Owatonna State Home for Homeless and Abandoned Children."

Doris and Albert both started to cry out loud.

IX

Summary of correspondence between Calen A. Marrill, Superintendent of the State Public School, W. E. Scott, Judge of the Probate Court, and Frank O'Malley—regarding the fate of the five youngest Norgren children.

May 9, 1930
A letter from Calen A. Marrill in response to a previous letter (May 8) from Judge W. E. Scott, suggests that the five younger siblings—Doris, Florence, Dougal, Albert, and Betty—be committed to the State Public School in Owatonna, with the State Board of Control as the children's official guardian. (Appendix B)

May 15, 1930

Judge W. E. Scott responds to Galen Marrill's letter (May 9), saying he thinks it is "very probable that the children will be committed to the State Public School at Owatanna," and would arrive the following week. Judge Scott continues, "There are four families here that have signified that they would like to each adopt one of the children." Mr. and Mrs. Frank O'Malley were interested in adopting Florence. Mr. and Mrs. William Hill "would provide well for a child…. I would most heartily recommend that Betty be placed with them if they so desire." (Appendix C)

May 15, 1930

In his letter to Mr. Galen A. Marrill, Superintendant of the Minnesota State Public School in Owatonna, Minnesota, Frank O'Malley states that "Mrs. O'Malley and I are very anxious to adopt one of the little children, namely, Florence." Mr. O'Malley asks whether Florence might be permitted to return to Two Harbors with Mrs. O'Malley "at once…providing conditions are satisfactory?" (Appendix D)

May 16, 1930

The response to Mr. Frank O'Malley was typed and mailed back to him along with the blank application, which he was to fill out and return. He was also told that it was quite impossible to grant his request at this time as they had not yet received the commitment papers or the history reports of the children and then, of course, the return of his application for adoption must be reviewed. Every applicant's home must be visited by an agent before the approval process could be finalized.

May 17, 1930

An Application for a Child from the State Public School was filled out by Frank O'Malley and Mrs. Pearl O'Malley. Intent: To give Florence a home. The O'Malleys report that they live in an eight-room house in good condition. Florence would have her own bedroom. They also reported that Frank's nationality (a question on the application) is Irish and that he is fifty-two years old and in good health. As asked on the application, his wife is forty-five years old, her nationality is German and in good health and they have been married for fifteen years. The names and ages of their children living at home was "no children." Florence Norgren was eleven years old.

JUVENILE COURT, FINDINGS AND ORDER
THE STATE OF MINNESOTA, COUNTY OF LAKE
May 19, 1930

In the matter of Doris Norgren, Florence Norgren, Dougal Norgren, Albert Norgren, Betty Norgren. (All their file numbers are handwritten near their names.)

The above entitled matter came on regularly for hearing before the said Court on the 19th day of May, 1930 at 10 o'clock a.m. before the Honorable W. E. Scott, Judge of said Court, upon the petition of Mrs. John Sandwick, duly filed herein, said children are being represented at said hearing; Mrs. John Sandwick, the custodian of the children, was also present as well as Miss Nellie Swanson, welfare worker of the Duluth, Missabe & Northern Railway Co., who has made thorough investigations in the matter.

And it appearing to the court that all person entitled thereto have had due and sufficient notice of these proceedings according to the statue in such case made and provided; and the court having heard all the evidence adduced at said hearing, and being fully advised in the premises, make the following FINDINGS OF FACT:

That said Doris Norgren, Florence Norgren, Dougal Norgren, Albert Norgren and Betty Norgren. are dependent children and that the allegations of said petition are true.

That said Doris Norgren, Florence Norgren, Dougal Norgren and Betty Norgren were born at Knife River, Minnesota on Dec. 7, 1916; Aug. 5, 1918, July 6, 1920; and Jan. 15, 1925 respectively; and that Albert Norgren was born at Two Harbors, Minn. On July 19, 1922.

That the father of said children is dead, whose mother of said children is insane at the Wilmar State Hospital.

IT IS THEREFORE ORDERED, That said children be and they are hereby declared, adjudged and determined to be dependent children that said children be and they are hereby committed to the care and guardianship of Minnesota State Public School at Owatonna, Minnesota. County of Steele and State of Minnesota, and that said children shall there remain until they shall attain their majority unless sooner discharged by due course of law or by competent authority.

          By the Court:
          signed by: W. E. Scott, Judge.
          Two Harbors, Minn. May 19, 1930

June 21, 1930

A letter from Mr. Jager, State Agent in Owatonna to the Judge of Probate in Two Harbors stated that he had been hoping to bring some of the children back to his city this week. However, they had all been exposed to chickenpox and the two youngest were in the hospital and must be there for some time. He planned to bring Florence next week, "as she is in good condition."

Part 2
My Search: The Knife River

I

Summer 2010

I sit at my writing desk in the treehouse-like portion of my one-bedroom apartment, at the age of fifty-three. My research, still in progress to unravel this story, fact from fiction, memory by memory, is driven by my desire to work out the inherited trauma that permeates my existence daily. Shame mixed with intrigue, an obsession to understand what really happened with my biological grandmother to cause her to do what she did, and to find some compassion and forgiveness for her husband, my grandfather who seems to have abandoned us all.

Then it hits me. I know it's time to read that damn historical marker. Right now, on this sunny summer day. Grabbing my leather backpack that I use as a camera case, and my purse, I'm off, running down the two flights of stairs to what feels like a major source of freedom. I can handle it now. It is time for me to know exactly what it reads.

II

Summer 1969

It's coming up. The historical marker that my mother talks about every time we drive by. We have not stopped at this wayside rest, ever, as a family. That brings me to a belief, deeper in me than can be identified, that if there was nothing to be ashamed of, we would stop and read it, discuss and hear the whole story.

I study the landscape, as we fly by, looking out of the large side window of my family's yellow Ford station wagon. My dad is driving and my mom is sitting in the front seat. "Here comes the hysterical marker," she says with glee, turning to smile at us to see if we get it that she is making a play on words "and there's the little house where I was born. See…….here it comes……, right…….there! That little yellow house, that's where mama was born," she exclaims for the millionth time, pointing her finger as we zoom on by.

My forehead pushes against the window as we fly by at 45 miles per hour. I can't see inside that house, but everything inside me longs to, so I can understand. I'm sure there must be answers in there to all my questions.

My two younger sisters and my baby brother seem unaffected by it all, but for me, this drive, and the connection it has to our horrible family history, is painful and I never can understand why she tells it with such joy. I must be the only one who feels it.

III

Summer 2010

As I drive the ten miles up the North Shore of Lake Superior, I realize how far I've come in the telling of this story and realize that it is time for me to see the truth. Time for me to verify what I already know: that the words, the story etched in stone and metal of the Historical Marker Rest Area of the Knife River, is not about me or my dark family history.

My heart is beating so hard. I remind myself that I am an adult, nothing bad is happening now. I'm free and happy and on an adventure. I turn to the right, in my reliable, comfortable and ever so popular, green Subaru Forester. This puts me on the Knife River Frontage Road, just a few hundred yards to the parking lot, but the house is to my left. There it is. It's blue now and I cruise by, not ready to stop in, asking if I can see the inside of their home, whoever lives there now. Just to the marker for now, that is enough. Parking, grabbing the camera and there I stand before it, reading.

Very uneventful. It's a marker to tell the story of how the freeway was decided on and came to be. It's about the freeway.

NOW TO THE river. As I start to walk away from the marker, I look to my left. The house is just a few hundred yards northeast. I can't see it for the trees, but I know it's there. Turning again to my right and walking just a few yards, I see a very wide, and surprisingly long, beautifully built wooden stairway that looks like it will safely take me down to the river. I take a deep breath, grab the rail, and walk down, for the first time in my life, to see if I can find the spot, the place where it all came crashing down for my mother and her sisters and brothers, and mostly, for my grandmother, who was at the end of her ability to cope or to fight for herself and her children any longer. I wondered if I would know by the look of it or by the feel of it. I wanted to know it. I wanted to meet it and make a friend or enemy of it. I was not sure which.

Down my feet landed and there I was at the river. I was taken aback by how close to the bottom of the stairway it was. My feet took me to the left, I hesitated but no, the house was over that way, and that was the way to go. Moving along this nondescript, unimpressive, skinny little path with the long grasses and deciduous trees here and there, the hill rising quickly to my left now, but my focus is the water. This river of my blood, my skin, my breath moving very slowly and gently beside me.

Less than four steps into my journey and I'm here at the river's edge with my feet searching for the most stable place to stop and touch the water. Most of me is disappointed. There is no high bank on the other side, the one I had pictured in my telling of the story. With the water so slow and easy, traveling by on its short way to the lake, I was sad to know this was not the place I thought it was. My eyes searched for clues, though I had no way of knowing what they were. Still I thought I might know. I had it in my head that the water had to have been rushing and deep enough to have really been a means to a drowning or two. My heart and imagination had been here so many times before, this obscurity was a bit maddening.

My walk took me further north on the trail, but it ended so quickly. I was sure this couldn't be all of it. I could not see the house up above, only thick brush and trees. I climbed over the dirt barrier, or more like a pile of dirt, that grass had been thriving on for quite a while. I stepped onto the road that U turns back toward the populated, if you can call it that, part of town and closer to the mouth that pours into the largest of the Great Lakes.

It wasn't right. I was moving away from the important area; I could feel that. So I stepped back over the bump and walked past the gentle widening of the river where I had just squatted before. This led me away from any sense of place. I had no idea how I would ever know where it was, exactly. I had to settle with that, and sitting on a rock, near my first touch of the water, I let myself rest on what I had come to do. I had read that ridiculously benign historical marker and I felt it all to be hysterically funny after all. I had to giggle, or I would cry. I thanked my mom and walked back to my car.

IV

I drove around the parking lot to go back down the frontage road looking again at the now blue house, wondering if I would ever have the courage to knock on the door and ask to see inside. I turn right to take me back into the tiny town of Knife River, Minnesota, finding as many drivable roads near this river as I can, trying to identify where along the shore it happened. I look for any sign of a path that would have led my family down to the river from my grandmother's house above. I slowly drive along the dirt road that runs along the north side of the water feeling as though this excursion might bring neither closure nor new information. Starting to feel hopeless and lonely in my pursuit, I notice two people working in the yard to my right and the woman looks up and smiles and waves hello so I decide to be brave and stop to ask. They are about my age or maybe a bit older and I know the blue house is close by, if the road continues, I would say less than a city block and up on the ridge to the right.

"Hi," I hollered. The woman walked toward me with a pleasant smile and the sincere desire to be helpful.

"Hi," she replied. "How can I help you?"

"Hi," nervously came out of me again. I always have big fears about intruding. "I am looking for any information about a tragedy that occurred here around 1928," I reported, leaning way over toward the passenger side window that I had opened with the push of a button. "My grandmother was said to have taken her eight children down to the river."

And before I could go on, the stranger finished my sentence. She knew. My body went numb and my brain sharpened all at once. I forced myself to focus and listen and begged myself not to be shy and hurry away. "That was your Grandmother?" she asked with a sadness and excitement all at once. By this time her husband had come over, hearing the conversation, and said, "I remember that. My parents spoke of it; that is all I know."

The woman spoke at the same time, wishing she had more to tell me. She too had only heard it spoken of by parents and friends. "Do you have any idea in which part of the river it happened, or of anyone who is still living that might know more?" I asked. My body was jumping ahead, like always, wanting to be done with the conversation, never knowing how to just be with people and talk and listen, my fears busting my ability to enjoy conversation with others.

My insecurities were screaming in my ears but my mission was clear and I was being handed some hope, so I paid attention. The woman looked at her husband, as if surprised that I didn't know. "Ya" he said, "it's just up the river. If you drive up to the frontage road." He pointed back the way I had come, "just back that way a bit and take a left, the frontage road is just before the freeway. You take a left on that and drive right up to the Rest Area there."

"I know that marker, I know where that is," I said, nodding and wishing.

"Well, it's that little area right at the bottom of the stairs. Chub pond is what they call it. Just to the left of the bottom of the stairs, right there." He looked at his wife, she looked at me.

"I was there," I said, with such doubt, "but it's so calm and shallow," the question came clear.

"Well" he said, "that's cuz it hasn't rained in a long while. After a rain, that river roars and that pond gets pretty swift and deep out in the middle of it."

The woman said excitedly, "You know what, there are a couple of people that are still alive that might have some information for you. There is Gloria, just up the side street here, right on the road. A little white house with a garage that faces the road. You can just go knock on her door. I think she knew your aunt, went to school with her. Didn't you have an Aunt Flossy?"

"I did, yes," I said. "I'll go see her."

"And then there is a house almost directly across from Kendall's smoked fish store. Do you know where that is?" she asked.

"Yes, of course," I answered.

"You knock on that old man's door too. He may have some information for you." she added.

"All right," I said. "This is great! Thank you so much! Thank you," I said again.

"Good luck," they said. "Glad you stopped." Stunned, I kept driving up to the dead end of the road. I saw the pile of overgrown dirt I'd walked over and knew just how close I really was again to the pond. Really? This place of horror and curiosity for me is called Chub Pond? Not a great name for a crime scene.

History of the Town of Two Harbors

"Minnesota's Trunk Highway 61 runs northeast out of Duluth along Lake Superior's rugged north shore. Before the 1920s, no reliable road ran through this area, a wilderness until the late nineteenth century. A string of towns, once hardscrabble fishing villages, were founded by Norwegian immigrants who toughed out the brutal winters because they were reminded of home. Smoked fish shops still edge the road, but quaint restaurants and antique shops have replaced general stores. Visitors needed to pack an above-average sense of adventure before the road brought a modicum of amenities.

At Agate Bay, a rare, natural harbor on Lake Superior's treacherous, rock-fringed north shore, history takes material form on a giant scale. Steel for the car you drive, the structure of the building where you work, and the grommets on the shoes you wear might contain iron ore transshipped at Two Harbors. Iron ore proved to be the diamond in the rough for nineteenth-century prospectors searching for gold, silver, and other minerals.

Three iron ranges stretched across northern Minnesota, but the ease of open-pit mining made the Mesabi Range the mother lode. Railroads soon radiated from the mines, one terminating at Agate Bay, which, together with the adjacent Burlington Bay, gave a name to the community that sprang up at the port: Two Harbors.

Lake Superior is the biggest, deepest, coldest, and wildest of the Great Lakes. Duluth is the country's furthest inland ocean port. Two Harbors is about twenty-two miles closer to the Atlantic. The vessels in the harbor are called ore "boats," a diminutive term given the mammoth scale of these freighters. Their routes are predictable: Haul taconite to the steel mills of Ohio and Pennsylvania, then deadhead back for another load of taconite. Any trip, though, is subject to the foul whims of Lake Superior. The Edmund Fitzgerald (immortalized in folk song) is only one of hundreds of wrecks littering the lake's cold bottom.

The first dock in Two Harbors, put into service in 1884, was 550 feet long and 40 feet high, could hold some 3,000 tons, and was made of wood.

The sixth dock rose in 1908—the first reinforced-concrete and steel ore dock in the country and one of the first in the world. Expected to last twice as long as the 12-year life of a typical timber structure, Dock No. 6 still hovers above Agate Bay, although it was decommissioned in the 1970s. Its even more massive concrete and steel neighbors, which replaced timber Docks No. 1 and 2 in the 1910s, remain in service.

Two Harbors had always been a company town, with nearly 95 percent of the community's workforce employed by the railroad by 1900."

Source: Charlene K. Roise. April 2005. Landscape Architecture Magazine. *What's in store for the aging industrial landscape of Agate Bay? Vol. 95, No. 4. pp. 118-123.*

**Part 3
The Orphanage**

I

May 1930, Betty Lois

We pulled up in front of "the cottage," as Miss Nellie called it. She told us to stay in the car until she returned, but as soon as she got to the door, there were two people coming out to her. They talked for a long, long time and finally came to the car and invited us in. Dougal wanted to make sure we were all going to stay together. Flossy and Doris assured him we would. Flossy read the name at the top of the door. "The Sunshine Cottage" she said. I liked the sound of that and hoped that breakfast would be awaiting us, hoping for one like the one we'd been given before we left.

Flossy and I looked out at the big brick buildings with lights in the windows and held each other tighter than ever. In a very soft message, so quietly it felt mostly to herself, Flossy said "Maybe things will be better here?"

"HELLO BETTY," SHE said to me, with a fake and scary grin. Her eyes did not smile at all. Her eyes were gray with dark brown circles underneath. She had dark brown hair all pulled up in a knot at the top of her head. Some of the curled pieces were falling down away from her knot and seemed to be pushing themselves as far away from her as they could get. She took my little hand and roughly pulled all thirty-six pounds of me to my new room. There were two rows of beds on each side of the room. Each row had six little beds made of thick white iron pipe and white sheets and blankets.

Miss B. let go of my hand roughly and told me my bed was #11. I looked at the beds but could not tell which one she meant. I did not know how to read numbers yet. She stood with her hands on her hips and her face looking like punishment if I didn't find my bed. I started to walk, very slowly, down the row of beds and looked at each one with such care, thinking that since it was my bed, I should be able to find it. My feet went flying up off the ground as she yanked my elbow hard, with the "Why?" that came screaming out of her mouth.

My skin and my head felt instantly hot and my ears rang with fear. I was facing her now and she was asking me something. I could not understand what. I could only hear the muffled sounds of her angry voice and I could see her getting angrier as my tears flowed down my face and my head and face got hotter and hotter. The next thing I remember was opening my eyes to see the white ceiling. My heart was racing as I moved only my eyes to see where I was, hoping I was home. In my head was a constant stabbing, like a piece of sharp glass poking me from inside. I felt the suffering of it in my eyes, my ears, my neck and in my stomach. It was horrible and I was so alone with it. I couldn't move. I knew if I did, it would get worse. I lay there for a bit but could not remember where I was, so I decided to turn over on my side, very carefully. Seeing the other beds and the white walls reminded me, so I curled up, within my pain, for two days.

II

No breakfast. First we were separated, sisters from brothers and guided into the scrubbing rooms. We were stripped naked and set into tubs to be scrubbed like animals. No mercy. I screamed and cried, as did my sisters, as the mercilessly strong women scrubbed our delicate skin with soap and brushes. Our hair was yanked of its snarls and scalped by the hard bristle brushes. The rinsing tubs were no better. The sting of disinfectant and the smell of burning flesh made me so sick, my head started to pound. The subsequent rinse tubs became less painful as we went. The women who washed us said nothing. They did not look us in the eyes, they did not seem to hear our cries.

III

No one would let us see our brothers. Doris, Flossy and I were all kept in the Sunshine Cottage for two weeks. We were examined and asked questions about our health and our family. Mostly we were asked about our mom and dad. I was just five and a half and really did not understand what was happening. I was sure that things would be going back to normal pretty soon, even though Doris told me all the time that they wouldn't. "Things are completely changed now Betty, I'm telling you," she would say as she shook her head up and down and then side to side like she knew everything. "Nothing's ever going to be the same again." And she was right.

I would look to Flossy to see if Doris was telling the truth. Flossy would wink at me and smile. She would tell me, when Doris was busy yapping with some of the other girls in detention, that she thought things would come back around to good. "I'm not sure when," Flossy would whisper, "but they will, I'm pretty darn sure."

I believed what Flossy told me much more often than I ever would believe what Doris told me. Doris could change her mood in an instant. She was funny and happy and then it would change. It made me nervous not to know who she was going to be from minute to minute. Kinda like Mama. She reminded me of Mama. Mama was always mad at Pa and so was Doris. Flossy said that they both had good reason to be but didn't ever go into it any further with me.

When our two weeks were up, we thought we would be seeing our brothers, but, as we were being assigned to our cottages, we were not even allowed to be together. Doris, Flossy and I were separated, and they told us it was best for being placed in good homes. I was put into cottage #4 and I didn't know where they put my sisters. I was all alone without any of my family. I was all alone with my new Matron, Miss B.

IV

I felt someone touching my back and shoulder, not too hard though, which I was so grateful for, and then I was being moved. I remember voices talking about how thin and small I was.

Back home, when I got this way, my papa would not leave me alone. He didn't believe that it hurt so bad I could barely breathe. He hit me in my terribly pain-filled head, so often. There were days when I was completely unable to come down for meals or go to school, though when I was made to, the nurse let me stay on her cot for hours putting cold compresses on my head and neck. I remember my pa yelling to our housekeeper, Mrs. Sandwick, as I was crouched on the floor in front of him, in the kitchen. "She is a dirty little faker. She is to do the dishes on her appointed days no matter what she whines about!"

Mrs. Sandwick would say: "You are not immune from the chores of this household, Betty Lois, you need to help your sisters do the dishes."

"Ahhhh," is all that I could get out of my mouth. Everything seemed so far away in my pain, confusing me and often making me vomit.

"If you throw up you'll be the one cleaning up!" Mrs. Sandwick would say as she left the room. I did clean it up, but she helped me do so, quite often. As she moved out of the room, I did my best to help, and my sisters did their best to help me make it through, until I could get up the stairs, settling into the darkness and depth of my pain.

V

As I waited to be released from the hospital ward, I thought of my sisters and brothers, recalling the smiles and the fights, the singing and dancing and the times when we would hide from our papa in the woods. I could run real fast when I had to, but Doris didn't run very well. She had a hard time with her feet and hands; her whole body moved differently. She was slow, Mama said, sweet but slow, and too easy for Papa to catch.

I WAS SENT back to my cottage to live with Miss B. and the other girls. Miss B. didn't like me much, but she seemed not to bother me so much after that. I did what I was told, I stayed out of her way and she pretty much stayed out of mine most of the time.

I did make two good friends who lived in my cottage. We would meet outside on the playground and talk about matrons and how life was for us in our cottage. Molly was just one year older than I, and Ella Baker, she was a colored girl, almost the exact same age as I was. She was just as nice to me as anyone could be. She and I had many fun hours of friendship, playing pretend, and making funny faces at each other while we sat on the very hard wooden chairs in the basement.

I started to wonder why I never got to see my sisters after a few weeks went by. I knew Doris and Flossy were here, but I didn't see them. Not on the playground, not at lunch or dinner.

"Molly," I said to my friend, "I don't ever see my brothers or my sisters around here." She looked at me like I was crazy.

"And you're never going to," she said.

"Why not? What do you mean?" Her answer was full of anger.

"We do not have families anymore, Miss B. says. She says it is much easier to place children that are lonely, like us," as she pointed back and forth from her to me about five times. I told her she was annoying me and walked away just as fast as I could. My tears and fear would not wait. I never did ask Miss B. I just did not want to have a reason to hate her even more.

SOMETIMES WE PLAYED outside for half the day, when it really wasn't very warm or dry. Our outdoor clothes often were not sufficient. I was not there for the winter months, but over the years, I heard from my sisters and brothers that winter was brutal and punishments often included sitting in cold spaces, sometimes outdoors. There were people that gave us love at the orphanage, but sadly they were few and far between. Some of the house matrons, from what I heard, were loving and kind but very tired and overburdened. Truth be told, most were cruel and abusive. They lived there with us twenty-four hours a day, seven days a week. How sad for all of us.

On my first morning there, after I got out of the hospital, we were marched down to the basement right out of bed. In the basement of each cottage were as many chairs as were children. Wooden chairs of varying size. It was made very clear that if we did not follow instructions while in this room, and sit perfectly still on our designated chair, we would be severely punished.

One day, for me, that meant sitting on that chair for the entire morning, in the corner, not moving, not turning to look at the other groups of children and matrons that were coming and going. I had to just sit there on the very uncomfortable, too big for me, feet dangling, hard wooden chair. It had been dragged right up next to, and was facing, that ugly dull corner of the room. When the room was empty, I would move around on the chair trying to find some comfort, and I even slightly stood up a few times just to get feeling back in my legs, always fearful of being caught. But I wasn't, and I survived it and learned my way around the basement chair room rules. I looked forward to the day when I could forget those chairs. It felt like a cruel game was being played on us, while we were sitting on them.

VI

While being prepared to leave the orphanage, Betty was instructed by the orphanage placement officer that she was never to speak of or communicate with her past family members. She was told that if she should happen to see them out in the world anywhere, she was to turn and walk away. She was being given to a new family now and must obey and honor them.

Her old family no longer existed, and they had been given the same rules. She was told that she was very fortunate to be chosen by such an important family and if she failed to follow this strict rule, she could be sent back to the orphanage to live forever. Betty deposited this information into her already bruised and tender heart as she was loaded onto a bus, with her small orphanage-issued suitcase and was driven the two hundred sixty miles to her new family's home. She had ten hours to process this round of the bruising of her heart and the mapping of her brain to loss and abandonment. She'd had much to face in her first five years of life, now living in her sixth and being placed.

**Part 4
New Name, New Life**

I

Betty had been delivered, via the orphanage bus, to her new home on a cold winter afternoon. The driver let her off at the curb of Eighth Avenue, Two Harbors, and pointed up the side-yard walkway to the back porch. Betty clumsily carried herself and her little suitcase up to the porch and looked back at the bus driver for further instructions. She wanted to run back onto the bus but she had her instructions and no other options, so she followed his hand signals and climbed the six stairs to the back door. Once again looking for direction, she knocked and waited. Thinking that the house was grand and beautiful, her mind started to wonder about her new life.

Then the door opened and there, with her hand on her hip, was a mean-looking face with a hand coming toward her. Betty was grabbed by the shoulder and dragged inside, with the door quickly closed behind her. With no greeting or kind words from this large and angry woman, Betty was led through the inner back porch filled with gardening pots and tools, then through another door that landed them in the kitchen. She caught glimpses of the warm room, with green walls and a large white stove. A friendly table and chair sat in the center of the room. "Sit down," Edna said gruffly. Betty climbed onto the chair that sat next to the door and watched as her boots were unlaced, pulled off and placed on the rug next to her.

Without warning she was once again being pulled by the shoulder of her coat, out of the kitchen and through another room that she, by cranking her neck, was able to determine was the dining room. Moving quickly past a large dark, almost black and very fancy dining table and chairs, she noticed lacy curtains on the large windows across the room. With her face being forced toward the wall, she was now passing a bedroom with a fancy dark wooden bed and dressers. Then another short walk before they were passing through another room with a couch and a large green plant next to a beautiful big window.

She could hear another door being opened and was pushed into a small and very cold room, with a little bed to her left. The hold on her coat was released and she turned quickly to look once again at this warden who was telling her to unpack her suitcase and put her clothes in the dresser. The door was left open and the woman walked away back toward the kitchen.

Betty looked at the dresser that had been placed along the wall to the right of the door and felt the bitter cold coming through the throw rug that was under her stockinged feet, so she slid herself up on the edge of the bed, still clothed in coat, hat and mittens, and scooted herself back to lean against the wall that she noticed was also very cold. She was too stunned and frightened to move. As she sat looking at her new room and thought back on what she had seen in the rest of the house she noticed the sock doll that her mama had made her. It was propped against the pillow to her right. The doll that she was told would be waiting for her when she came home from the orphanage. Her heart leapt and sank all at once as she held it to her face and cried ever so quietly. She kept watch on the door, listening to the sounds this woman was making, too terrified to move.

Edna returned after a few minutes and scolded her for not minding, while she took the sock doll from her hands and put it back on the pillow. She roughly removed her hat, mittens and coat. Pushing the hat and mittens into the sleeves of the little coat and folding it over her arm, she grabbed Betty by her left ear and pulled her to the dining room toward a very large dark mahogany dining room chair. She climbed into the big dark chair while rubbing her ear and trying hard not to cry. Sitting short and small at the table, Betty looked directly level with the rim of a large plate that had been set before her. The word "eat" had been spoken before the room was empty and still.

Hungry as heck, little Betty reached up to a quartered piece of the huge sandwich and bit into the most wonderful chicken sandwich made with the sweetest homemade brown bread she had ever tasted. As the mayonnaise dripped down her chin, she tried hard to eat slowly and lady-like, as she had been taught by her sister Flossy when they were occasionally allowed to dine together at the orphanage. After staring into the bitten parts of her first piece of sandwich, she wiggled to find her footing on the rung of the chair, lifting herself enough and smiling to see the large glass of milk next to her plate. Leaning forward with her chin touching the rim of her sandwich plate, her eyes grew larger yet to see a small dish to the right that cradled a soft, fat, golden cookie so big that it almost filled the plate, and it sparkled with brown sugar on the top. This chair would become her place at the table for the remainder of her time with the Hills.

Betty loved the food that her new mama cooked and delighted at wearing the clothing; dresses and hats, slacks and blouses, jackets and coats that her new momma sewed for her. She came to love her little room, which was in fact the barely protected but enclosed front porch of the one bedroom first floor portion of the duplex the Hills owned and occupied. There was no basement under that little porch, just three walls filled with single pane windows and a roof, connected to the main house. At times what kept her cheerful when the going got tough were the daintiest cream-colored linen curtains she had ever seen. They hung from the windows in her room and were covered with pink, yellow and blue flowers with soft green intertwined stems and dancing leaves, handmade for her by her new momma.

From the front of the house, the enclosed porch was charming with a beautiful oak door that had a large oval window, but it was not meant to be lived in year-round. Betty had her challenges feeling safe and comfortable during extreme weather situations. For Betty the world was as good as it could be for she had a new home and she was determined to show her new family that she was obedient and well-behaved enough to be loved.

May 19, 1930. *Summary of child history forms completed for Betty Lois Norgren at the time of her placement with Bill and Edna Hill*
> Betty is described as being in good condition when examined by the school nurse. She was committed to the Owatonna State Public School on May 19, 1930, with the Cause of Dependency listed as "Death of father," and the Contributory Cause listed as "Insanity of mother." When admitted, her physical condition was also listed as "good," and that she had already had whooping cough, mumps, measles and scarlet fever, as reported by Doris and Florence. She was 41.5 inches tall and weighed 36 pounds. (Appendix E)

August 2, 1930. *Agreement between the State Board of Control and William M. Hill (Excerpts)*
> This Agreement.... placing Betty Lois Norgren, one of the wards of this Board, in the family of William M. Hill to remain until the 15th day of January 1943, when said child will be 18 years of age... maintaining, educating and treating her properly and kindly as a member of his family, to provide her with suitable and sufficient clothing for week days and for attending public religious worship and with suitable food and other necessaries in health and

sickness: to have her taught an occupation to enable her to become self-supporting and the branches usually taught in the common schools causing her to attend the public school where he resides fully complying with the compulsory school laws of Minnesota." (Appendix F)

At the age of five, after more than three years of living completely without her mother and a few months not seeing her sisters or brothers during her time at the state run orphanage and school, Betty Lois Norgren was placed into the home of assistant chief of police, William Hill, of Two Harbors, Minnesota, the same assistant chief of police that had come to the Norgren family home in Knife River to assist in removing Betty's mother from the rest of the family. He was also involved in trying to find homes for the eight children that had been under the care of the now deceased John Otto Norgren. I'm quite sure everyone knew John did not care for them since his wife had been institutionalized, nor had he before she died. He was a horribly miserable, alcoholic and violent man.

II

Bill and his wife Edna had not been blessed with children of their own and Bill had longed to be a father. Edna had been willing and even a little excited to have her husband's child but was incensed at being made to raise a child from such a poor and "crazy" family. Edna had settled nicely into her daily routines of preparing meals for herself and her husband, often sharing them with Bill's sister who lived in the apartment upstairs. Edna had become quite an expert seamstress and her gardens were the talk of the town. She enjoyed her busy and creative time at home alone and within the community.

Edna plunged into an irritable state of mind after having this new responsibility thrust upon her. She was never asked by Bill if she would be happy to do this. She had only been directed by Bill and his sister Nan, to become the mother this child had lost to the insane asylum. She went through the motions of parenting but showed no love or pleasure in having this small female child plunked into her home and life. Betty was very aware of how unwelcome she was but with no understanding of the adult situation, was quite sure it was because she was not acceptable.

November 10, 1932. *Letter to Dr. William F. Smith of the Wilmar State Hospital from Phyllis M. Zamboni, Child Placing Agent at the Minnesota State Public School*

> My Dear Dr. Smith:
>
> Upon the request of the foster parents of Betty Norgren, ward of this institution, I am writing you for a report of the condition of Betty's mother, Mary Norgren, aged 44 who was committed to the Wilmar Hospital about 1928.
>
> We should appreciate a summary of the patient's social medical history—with a statement of the mental diagnosis upon admission, subsequent changes in diagnosis, her response to treatment, and the present prognosis.
>
> Thank you for your helpfulness. (Appendix G)

November 12, 1932. *Response from Dr. William F. Smith, Superintendent of the Wilmar State Asylum to Phyllis M. Zamboni, Child Placing Agent at the Minnesota State Public School*

Dear Madam:

Your letter of November 10 concerning Mrs. Mary Norgren has been received. She was committed to the Fergus Falls State Hospital in September 1926. The date of her birth is 1887. She attended the 5th grade in school and her religion is protestant. Her mental diagnosis is Dementia Praecox, Hebephrenic type. Her commitment history gives the following information and it is about 3 years and 7 months previous to admission to Fergus Falls.

> "First symptoms about one year ago. She was nervous and neglected her housework and children. Religious. Imagines some injury to her head. Threatened her children and husband. She was very religious. She was in the county jail for three days."

Fergus Falls State Hospital gives the following information on her while she was there.

> "On admission she was delusional, her delusions being of a sexual nature. She had ideas that she had relations with her nine year old, girl, etc. She had ideas that her husband had relations with her nine year old daughter and that he was unfaithful and kept company with other women. She is listless, indifferent, shows no capacity for employment and scolds at times. Her sister Lillian Bucher is a patient at this hospital."

Her appetite is good and she sleeps well. She takes considerable interest in her surroundings and attends picture shows and chapel services at the institution. Her conversation is rambling and incoherent on some subjects. She continues to be delusional and at times will attack the nurses. Her present weight is 192 pounds. (Appendix H)

III

Flossy must have been accepted into the O'Malley home sometime after the above dated document. My mother told me that she worked very hard for the family, cooking, cleaning and taking care of Mrs. O'Malley from the moment she arrived. She was cared for, but from what my mom told me, she felt more like a servant. I don't remember ever meeting any of the O'Malleys as I was growing up, but Flossy and her husband Lorne were very involved in our lives. I don't remember ever being told how many other children the O'Malleys had, but Mrs. O'Malley was quite physically disabled and, I believe, was wheelchair bound. It seems to me that the children had all grown up and moved out by the time Florence got there at age eleven.

It took Flossy a month or two to settle in, learning all that her new family needed her to do. She was busy from early morning until she fell into bed at nine every night. Though they worked her hard from what I was told, Mr. and Mrs. O'Malley were kind to her and talked with her about the family she had before. Flossy was hesitant at first to converse about them but she came to believe that her new family really did care about how she was able to deal with those losses and changes.

One day, after telling Mrs. O'Malley that she was seeing her sister Betty at school, and once in a while would get to visit with her a bit, Mrs. O'Malley walked her to the front window and pointed, explaining how to get to the corner house two and a half short blocks away, adding "That is where your sister Betty now lives." Flossy looked at her new mother while she inhaled deeply with surprise.

Holding her breath, until she knew what to ask next. "Do I have your permission to see her?" Flossy asked.

"Yes," Mrs. O'Malley said, and added, "She needs you. But take your time, and be gentle with her and her new family."

Flossy nodded with joyful tears in her eyes, and promptly asked permission to take a quick walk to see the little green house with all the flower gardens around it. Mrs. O'Malley touched her new daughter's arm, to help her stay put for a moment and to tell her one more piece. "Yes, just to look from afar for now. Let things settle for a bit, and then, when we both agree that the time feels right, you can invite her to come for tea."

IV

It was a warm and sunny day and her strolls home from kindergarten were filled with wonder and adventure for the now six-year-old Betty Hill. She loved school and the walk home, much more than she loved reaching her destination. She was well-fed and kept very involved at home but her new mama and papa were not always gentle with her and they kept her at home and busy so she would not get into any trouble. She had seen Flossy at school, and they had carefully created a guarded relationship, but it was well known that Officer Bill Hill was on patrol and everyone knew everyone else, so caution was very necessary. The fear of being caught and believing that she could very well be sent back to the orphanage weighed heavy. Being a good girl was not an option that also carried that weight.

She was just a half block from home one day, when she heard someone running toward her from behind. Before she knew it a tall, blonde boy was standing right in front of her and looking down at her. He moved his arm up and gestured for her to take what was in his hand. She recognized the small triangular shaped piece of paper as something she had seen at school being passed between the older students, never having received one herself. "This is from your sister Flossy," he said, quickly pulling both her little hands up and together with her palms at heart level. He then gently placed the triangle note in the cup of her hands and ran off as fast as he'd come.

Betty stared at the note, knowing this was not allowed. Hearing the threat of punishment swirling in her mind was directly followed by the purity of understanding that she would be reading this note. They had been sneaking smiles at each other in the halls of school and carefully touching hands or elbows and sharing sweet words when they could. This was her beloved sister that cared for and loved her the best she could ever remember being loved.

Turning her back to the street, trying to hide from anyone's view, she unfolded the paper and the beautiful handwriting was clear. "PLEASE COME TO THE BACK DOOR FOR TEA." No signature.

She knew where the O'Malley house was and in no time at all Betty was standing at the O'Malley's back door, looking down at her shoes, waiting for the courage to knock. She looked up as the door began to open and there stood Flossy, her entire face a loving smile. She was invited in and after a hug that lasted a lifetime, she was seated at a table in the kitchen to drink tea and eat cake with Flossy.

They were sneaky and careful praying the Hills would never know, but would meet every day to touch, to talk a little, and to be happily reconnected. She was told that she would always be welcome at the O'Malley home.

V

February 26, 1931. *Excerpts from State Agent's Report, Betty Norgren, Age 6*

7. Its moral condition is: good usually, has been quite a problem though and they had some trouble with her at school, but is improving.

12. Recommendations and remarks: Mr. Hill has woodworking machinery and makes small furniture for Betty - She has many nice things to play with — writing desk, kitchen cabinet - kitchen utensils - dolls - happy and many more nice things. They will not adopt Betty as so many of her relatives are insane. (Appendix I)

October 21, 1932. *Excerpts from State Agent's Report, Betty Norgren, Age 7*

1. Child's physical condition: Child eats and sleeps well - has plenty of outdoor play. Is 2 lbs. underweight. Dr. Burns of Two Harbors gives medical supervision.

3. Progress in school is: Rapid - grade ahead of her age - give help at home. Studies the 3rd grade.

7. Its moral condition is: Satisfactory. Parents are inclined to be overly anxious about her school progress.

8. Is it contented? Yes.

9. Is it liked by guardian? Immensely. So devoted they are jealous of her interest in others.

10. The guardian's treatment of child is: Try to give her the right training, and establish wholesome regular habits of living.

11. The general impression of the home is: Modern, well furnished home. Betty has her own room. Mrs. H. a good housekeeper.

12. Recommendations and remarks: Mrs. H. welcomed the visit as many problems have been weighing on her mind. She is eager to estrange Betty from her sister Florence who lives three blocks away. I pointed out that it was only natural that the sisters should be interested in one another, and the surest way to strengthen the bond between the children, which is the Hill's fear, is to place restrictions on the sisters seeing one another. Mrs. H. also wondered whether there any advantage to their postponing adoption until Betty is 12 years old to be sure her development will be normal. Betty has been given 2 mental tests and was slightly above average on both tests. I advised that her schoolwork too showed her to have more than average mentality and the possibility of her carrying any trait from the mother which would develop before she was an adult was very improbable. Mrs. H. requested a report on the mother's condition.

Betty has shown no signs of instability. Emesis? cleared up after a year in her foster home. Mrs. H. asked my advice regarding having Betty repeat 3rd grade so she would not advance too rapidly. Advised Mrs. H. to let school promotions go along naturally and let her pass if she showed a capacity for higher grade work.

Mrs. H. said Betty was a gay, happy child. She has a good disposition — is eager to please and responds well to praise. She tries to be helpful about the house. Child is very neat and clean about her personal appearance. (Appendix J)

April 27, 1935. *Excerpts from State Agent's Report, Betty Norgren, Age 10*

Betty Norgren is ten years old.

Child's physical condition is: very good now - looks well, slightly less nervous. Repeating the fourth grade at parents request.

Helps with housework, likes to help with baking.

Moral attitude is: good, there are never any complaints about her conduct.

The guardians' treatment of the child is: very good. They feel their responsibility and protect her in every way. They keep her at home and with them rather too close.

Betty's relatives are in the same community but Mrs. Hill doesn't favor having Betty mix with them. They were very angry last fall with Dougal, brother, and his foster parents drove up to see the sisters and they called Betty out of school and all spent the day at O'Malley's.

Betty has had severe headaches, bites her fingernails, gets dreadfully nervous if there is undue excitement, etc. And with the quiet life in the home, she is improving. School work is hard for her and they asked that she be failed this year so as to repeat the grade and not tax her too much. This was done and she is doing better. Mrs. Hill attends night school, takes French and Current Events and is interested in educational work. Mr. Hill is now Chief of Police.

M. Goodnick
State Agent

It makes me so sad that Betty repeated the fourth grade at the Hill's request as I too was held back, repeating the second grade when we were all moved from our Catholic school to the public school. That really tears a kid down.

Little Betty was being very controlled. I can understand their fears. The family she was truly a part of was a mess. She stayed close with Flossy. I'm not sure when Florence became Flossy but we always knew her as Flossy, or Saucy as we called her before our mouths could say it properly, and it stuck. We called her Auntie Saucy forever. She loved it and we loved her. She was the happiest adult of all of the children, I would say. She was kind and generous, gentle with all of us, her nieces and nephews. She had the most delightful smile of anyone I've ever known, and when she would wink at me, along with that smile, she could melt every iceberg on this planet.

December 18, 1936. *Excerpts from State Agent's Report, Betty Norgren, Age 11*

5. The child's moral attitude is: good girl

7. The guardian's treatment of the child is: very good

9. Recommendations and remarks: Betty is becoming a fine looking girl and very well mannered. She is lady like and polite, can sit down and visit and show an interest in other things besides her own doings. She still has headaches, Mrs. Hill calls them migrane [sic], and says the doctor says they are quite common among children born of parents who become insane.

Betty is not an especially good student but with help at home they see that she keeps up with her grade. She prefers the out door sports to studying while at home. Mrs. Hill is very exact and wants ot do just the right thing and so sees to it that the girl does some work at home around the house. She is also very much interested in church work, the whole family is, and just now all are working for Christmas. They showed me his work shop in the basement and all the toys he had ready for the big church party. He does unusually fine work and his toys and small pieces of furniture last for many years as they are made so substantial. Among the pieces he had ready were, small cedar chests, doll beds and cradles, kitchen cupboards and cabinets, tables, chairs, wagons, carts, and toys of all kinds. He makes for the church and on Christmas eve they are distributed to the poor families. The church gave him $10 this year for the material used.

This is an interesting home to visit although Mrs. Hill rather resents anyone coming in snooping around or bossing as she says some people call it. She is always very friendly but she shows that she feels they can care for the girl without advice. She does not have the girl visit the others of her own family who live around there and they think that she should be more intimate with them but she feels that she just doesn't have the time to keep up with all the girl's relatives and so they keep away from them. Betty sees her sister at school sometimes. (Appendix K)

When I got to line 7 on the above form, it gave me pause. "The guardian's treatment of the child is: very good."

In the long run, I believe it was good that Betty was taken in by my eventually adoptive grandparents. It was also good that she was adopted by the Hills, but it certainly was no cake walk for Betty. She told me stories of physical punishments and abuse. She told me at age sixteen, her father or her mother, now I've forgotten, slapped her across the face and she returned the blow. She also reported that they never hit her again after that. She suffered, just as most children do I believe, at the mercy of their earthly wardens. From what I can see and feel now, at age sixty-two, we can be blessed by all of our experiences with a deep understanding of the beauty of each and its useful presence in our lives, or we hide from the pain and discomfort of them and continue to suffer, carrying on the darkness rather than the light.

July 25, 1937. Excerpts from State Agent's Report, Betty Norgren, Age 12

    1. The child's physical condition is: very good, has very few headaches now.
    2. The child's work is: helps at home and this summer is working for a neighbor a few hours a day
    3. The child's moral attitude is: good girl
    7. The guardian's care of the child is: very good
    8. The general impression of the home is: good city home—child doing well
    9. Recommendations and remarks: Betty is a nice girl and getting along all right. She is very enthusiastic about earning money this summer and is helping out at a neighbors caring for a little child and doing light housework. She works about 4 or 5 hours a day. She gets $1.50 a week and is saving it. She won't spend it unless for something she needs, bought a rain cape lately.

    They reported that Florence, who was with Mr. and Mrs. O'Malley in Two Harbors, left their home the night she graduated from High School in June and went to Duluth to do housework. Her sisters and brothers were there to see her graduate and took her back to Duluth with them. Doris, who was with the grandmother at Knife River, is also doing housework in Duluth.

    The children are all trying to get together and don't seem to like it because the Hills do not let Betty visit with them as often as they would like. They want to keep her with them. (Appendix L)

I was stunned and concerned upon reading the reference to Florence in the July 22, 1937 visit notes above. How telling to leave the moment you graduate from high school. I had never heard this part of the history of my Aunt Flossy. It breaks my heart to think that she was so miserable at the O'Malley's to flee like that. I wish I could ask her about it all. She was my angel and the kindest human I've ever known. So gentle and good to us and yet a bit disconnected and sad but it showed so lightly that it was easy to miss. I miss you Aunty Saucy.

June 26, 1938. Excerpts from State Agent's Report, Betty Norgren, Age 13

> Betty is now thirteen: She is in eighth grade. Good girl, no complaints. Betty is growing up into a fine looking girl. She stays at home most of the time and helps with the housework and with the garden. The whole family seems to prefer home to visiting around. Mr. Hill, Policeman, works nights. Spends some time each day in his basement shop making furniture and children's toys. Mrs. Hill loves flowers and her garden and spends her time there. They do not visit the other Norgren children or relatives.
>
> Betty sees Florence occasionally. She (Florence) has returned to the O'Malley home in Two Harbors and is keeping house for Mr. O'Malley as his wife died last year. Betty has a good home and is satisfied and is content there. (Appendix M)

Florence (Flossy) went back to the O'Malley's after Mrs. O'Malley died. That was another stunning find.

October 31, 1939. *Excerpts from Home Visit Report*, Betty Norgren, Age 14

There was no school the afternoon I called at the house and Betty had been allowed to go with the other school girls for the afternoon and so I did not see her.

Mrs. Hill reports that Betty is doing well in school, and is a good girl and there are no complaints. She has lately been visiting with her sisters and brothers in the community and so has finally made some contact with them which was not approved of while she was younger.

The sister who lived in another home in Two Harbors, is now married and Betty visits her occasionally. The others of the family visit the married sister and then Betty is invited there too so she has a chance to see them all.

They say that Albert Norgren is with his brother Deerwood (sic) who is married and living in Duluth. (Appendix N)

VI

Betty used to ride her bike down to the waterfront, grab the mail bag from inside the Railroad office, run down to the dock to wait for and then jump onto the Edna G. Tugboat as it was motoring by, only to jump off again as they neared the dock which led to the building where the mail needed to be delivered. She did this every weekday I believe. I can't remember if it would pick her back up on the way back or not, and I don't know how old she was when she started or when she stopped. I only know that she spoke of it with such delight.

VII

I can still feel all the love in the house of the only maternal grandparents I'd ever known. The house was always clean and warm, beautifully arranged and filled with the creative skills of both Bill and Edna. It felt so pleasant, welcoming and full of goodies for us to feel and enjoy, play with and delight in, right from the hearts of these two good people. Though I do remember some of the harshness, the don'ts and the hard edges of my grandparents. My Grandpa Hill died when I was quite young so most of my memories are with only Grandma Hill. We learned to behave as best we could when in the household of Grandma Hill and as far as I can tell or remember, she loved us in her stiff and disconnected way. As she and we aged, she softened and came to appreciate having us as family. She never created a doubt within me regarding it.

Their yard was filled with magic delights no matter the season. Some were made of wood and metal that came from the basement, which I don't ever remember going down into. But I can still clearly see, and somewhat feel, the creamy white walls and red painted stairs and railings heading down to it. It was not a wide stairwell and it was from the kitchen of the lower part of the house leading up to the apartment above and down to the basement.

Down those stairs was Bill Hill's woodworking shop, and must have also housed the laundry. I know not what it was like, but what came out of that lower level, these wonders, made by his thick, strong hands were incredible, and can still be found in the yards of people all over Two Harbors. If you see a windmill, it may have been made by my grandfather. All of them with lights and spinning wheels of varying color, with intricately made houses of white or yellow. Some with wooden baskets to carry clay pots with flowering plants in them, staying upright all the way around, as the wheel turned. I'm sure there were many that I have never seen or noticed. I was too young and insecure to marvel at them then. He made wood into joy for many.

IN SUMMER, MY grandmother could be found with her house dress on, bent over and weeding her amazing vegetable and flower gardens. She was an excellent seamstress and gardener, and her home cooking was delightful.

What I remember most is the warmth, the feelings of comfort and joy as all seven of us came bustling in the back door and into the long slim, creamy white, antique and fully windowed entryway porch, and entering the kitchen by the doorway on the right. This entry ritual is warm and welcoming to remember, but we all knew our manners must be in place. It was a blessing to enter into my grandma's kitchen. The smells were full and rich, the lighting soft and warm, the colors welcoming and clean. The thickness of the love that had been collected, prepared, heated and fussed over for days still warms my heart and stirs my soul, and can make my mouth water.

After taking our outerwear off with Grandma, Mom and Dad's help to remove and hang or place on the mats, we were welcomed in, to smell the smells, see the familiar kitchen table, the gas stove that was just to the right of the door that led to the large and wonderful dining room with the dark wood table to the left with its ornate matching chairs. A beautiful buffet to its left. At the end of the long table were the windows to the Avenue, with lacy ruffled curtains in perfect order and lacy tatted doily cloths on small dark-wood decorative side tables.

We were allowed to gently play, in the small living room, with a deck of cards and such and if we wanted, we could play in the large front porch area, where my mother had had her bedroom, if I am remembering correctly. It was an unheated space, but the door could be left open to warm it while we were there. There were many lovely windows and a pretty door with a large oval window in the top portion. I thought it very fancy indeed. We were all enjoying our time while waiting for the table to be filled with delicious food and we were never disappointed.

My grandmother, Mary McNeill Norgren (right) *circa* 1925.

Mary McNeill Norgren and John Otto Norgren (left) and Lillie Butcher with (presumed) spouse (right).

Betty at three different stages of girlhood at the time she was living with Bill and Edna Hill. Not sure, but judging from hairstyles these may be arranged from youngest (top) to oldest (bottom).

Betty around age 13.

Betty with neighborhood friends (above).

Betty (third from left), with friends at summer camp.

Betty (left) with neighbor and best friend Suzy Weatherby (right).

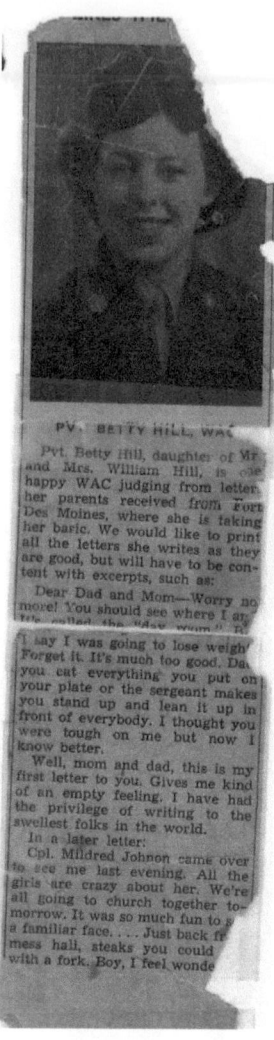

Women's Army Corps.

My mother, Betty Hill, joined the Women's Army Corps.

Betty in her Women's Army Corps uniform – including the required heels.

Betty (left) and the man she married, Walter (Tim) Wright, Jr.

Betty and Tim (center left, center right) on their wedding day with Betty's sister, Florence (left) and Florence's husband, Lorne (right).

Tim and Betty at home in Two Harbors, Minnesota.

Tim and Betty in Hawaii, where Tim was stationed at Pearl Harbor. Tim is holding baby Cathy.

Betty (right) fishing at the cabin on Bassett Lake near Brimson, Minnesota.

Betty (second from left) and girlfriends at Bassett Lake.

At the cabin on Bassett Lake. Betty (back row, second from left) and Tim (front and center). My parents' drinking friends varied over the years, though a few stayed close until their deaths, late in their eighties.

Have a beauty day!

Tim Wright.

Bill and Edna Hill.
May 11, 1958.

Grandpa Bill Hill with baby Cathy.

Grandma Edna Hill.
Cathy is on the right.

The photo above was sent to me via Ancestry.com from Karl Strom. 1215 Palmer Section House. Sandberg Norgren.

    The note on the emailed photo and description is that this photo was taken around 1912. It has been reported that the man with the pipe is Carl Arthur Sandberg and his brother, John Jr is on the far right. The back of the photo reports that Norgrens are included in this shot. A cousin named Mary Ann thinks that Betty (Norgren) Sandberg (Betty Lois' paternal grandmother) is the woman leaning in the doorway. The boy in the middle is most definitely a Norgren but the dates don't work for it to be one of my uncles if the date of this photo is correct. In 1912, John Otto Norgren was twenty-two or twenty-three years old and married Mary McNeill on February 25th, 1911. The boy in the middle might be a younger brother of John Otto, so would be one of my great uncles. He looks so mischievous, doesn't he? High cheekbones, beautiful smile and a handsome teenager.

Part 5
My Life Growing Up

I

We lived in a two-bedroom house on Avondale Street, Mom and Dad and my older sister, by seven and a half years. My bedroom was the first one to the right of the front door hallway, with the bathroom across the hall. I don't remember the rest of the house from there, but I'm guessing it was a two bedroom, so one more bedroom at the end of the hall. I think there was an attached garage on that end, with the short grass driveway.

My sister and I were both too young to be watching and learning while my dad and mom drank alcoholic beverages with what appeared to me to be such fun, ease and passion with many of their good friends. My parents' drinking friends varied over the years, though a few stayed close until their deaths, late in their eighties.

I remember them in the kitchen, joking, gossiping, laughing, singing, dancing, cooking, and eating. There were many gatherings in that little house. I have a photo of them all in the kitchen, with great grins on their faces looking pretty wasted, and that may be all there is to some of these memories. Why I don't remember them partying in the living room, I would venture to bet, was that they were either over at Dick and Val's house, just one house and a stroll across the avenue away, while my older sister babysat me or I was over there with them, as I do have slight memories of being in their living room. It is also possible that I had been put to bed for the night while they partied in the living room.

I do remember my dad coming back in after I'd been put to bed. I was crying, probably feeling afraid and all alone in my bedroom. He was standing mostly outside the door with it cracked open and telling me a bedtime rhyme: "Good night, sleep tight, and don't let the bedbugs bite, but if they do, take a shoe and hit them till they're black and," and he paused, finally saying "yellow" instead of "blue." I thought he was weird then, but knew he was trying to make me laugh and feel at ease. I was not yet three years old.

I HAVE A very clear memory of being in my dad's arms as he walked into our newly- purchased house on Pitt Street. He placed me gently down and walked away, leaving me in the center hallway that led to everywhere else in that wonderful old house. I stood there, looking around with delight. I remember that moment like it was yesterday.

After we moved to Pitt Street I don't remember seeing Dick and his kids as much. It was quite a bit further east and in a different school district, perhaps two miles away. Val died young and, if memory serves, while we were still living on Avondale. That was my first introduction to death. It made an impression. Her memory and her passing is an important part of me in some gossamer way. My senses were being honed by my mother's sadness and loss of a dear neighbor and friend.

There must have been a time of worry as she was diagnosed with cancer, but the treatments, in 1960, were not very promising. I wasn't capable of comprehending that part of this experience for my parents and Val's family, but the death, somehow, I knew. I sensed the deep loss and sorrow. I missed seeing her when they would gather. I felt her beautiful presence though she was gone. I can feel her love as I write this. The loss of Val Weatherby was deep for us all. It seems I have always been very spiritually curious.

II

As a teen, my dad, "Tim," as they called him, was president of the Pep Club and played football on the high school team. He played the drums in the school band and on into his eighties, though I don't remember him playing when I was growing up. He started up again later in life and played many gigs around town in a pretty big band, along with my youngest sister, Jen, who played the trumpet. I attended their events often to hear and watch them make music and be buddies. I watched and danced while he played in a ballroom style dance band in Florida, when my mom and he started their snowbird life.

As we all, my parents included, were growing up together, my dad's love of sports was honored and shared by most of the family. My dad played for many years for one of the local sports teams sponsored by Jeno Paulucci, a widely honored and locally loved self-made Duluth millionaire. We grew up watching dad play at Portman Square in the Lakeside neighborhood, at Wheeler field out in West Duluth, in the Woodland neighborhood ball fields and at Wade stadium. He played fast pitch softball playing first base and pitching, then when he got older, slow pitch, pitching and outfield.

There were so many things that didn't help my dad and me connect. Sports was one of them. I was a dancer and a gymnast, in our living room and outdoors until I started in junior high, practicing like crazy and so excited to try out to be a cheerleader. The day before tryouts, being known as a shoe-in and so excited to find my niche, my skill and talent as an athlete of sorts, I was practiced and ready. The night before, I started to have an extremely painful right upper thigh, along with swelling. I ended up in the hospital and missed the tryouts. I had a bacterial infection from getting dirt in the cracks that I often had on the soles of my feet and in between my toes. I was okay within a day or two but my Junior High would not allow me to try out. I lost big time, or so I thought.

I soon started hanging with the "dirt bags" as we were called, smoking and walking or hitch-hiking out to Lester Park to hang with the older "dirt bags." I was learning how to create my own way of life. I'd finally given up trying to fit into the family. It did involve some not so healthy or legal things to try. I wanted to feel okay, a welcomed part of a group and ignore my painful and confusing home, school and family. We all were gathering there to do the same. To try to be cool and loose, and have some fun and find some joy in each other and the natural surroundings of Lester Park.

I am still not anything like my siblings. Back then, when I was fourteen or fifteen years old and beyond, we rarely had a reason to be together, other than babysitting, fighting, cooking or cleaning. I moved out of my parents' home on my eighteenth birthday.

I did have a few years of playing softball with my younger, more athletic sisters, Donna and Jen. Though they both played in many higher stakes teams, for a couple of seasons when I was in my late twenties, they took me under their wings and let me play catcher on their city parks and women's team. I had a blast and surprised us all with my abilities to throw, catch, run, hit and outfield. I was no star but there were a few star moments for me in the two or three wonderful years I played with them.

My funniest and most terrifying non-star moment was when the bases were loaded, and the pitcher, Jen, let me know to get ready for a play at home base. I had my catcher's mask on and my glove at the ready to catch each pitch. Once the bat hit the ball, I knew I was in a position to "do something wonderful" as Betty would yell from the benches to all of the players. Poised to quickly remove my mask and toss it to the fence behind me, I tossed my glove instead and there I stood, with my mask on and no way to catch and tag the runner who was side-stepping toward home while watching the play of the ball. I was sunk. I stood there frozen, trying to decide if I should run for the mitt or stay and try to do this without it, my inexperience showing all so clearly. I got lucky and neither the play nor the runner was coming to home base. I didn't know until after the game was over that no one saw what I did.

That time of our sisterly lives was the best it would ever be for me. Though it was painful for me that Tim and Betty were only there for that one game while I was involved, in the stands of the softball fields at Wheeler, cheering us all on. They rarely missed any of my siblings' other softball, baseball, basketball or other sports games. I attended many sports events with my parents, cheering the rest of them all on.

Being part of a sports team was my attempt to fit in more with my jockish family. I longed to find ways to feel closer and more appreciated by my dad and sisters. I longed for them to see and know me, to love and find joy in my being. I was trying to see and know me, to love and find joy in my being. I didn't know how.

I still hold dear the memories of my sisters, carrying me up on their shoulders after I hit the winning run in. That can never be taken from me. I didn't know why all were cheering and running toward me as I stood on second base. I asked why they picked me up after they put me down at the dugout, and my total jock-sister Jen just laughed and shook her head, still smiling and explained. I don't know why all that fun fell apart, but it did. Most especially, after my mom started fading away with dementia and then dying. After that, we all fell away from each other, in one way or another.

One weekend day, I was invited to drive out to Jen's country home to make traditional holiday potica with her and Donna. I was thrilled by the invitation and looking forward to a lovely time with my sisters. This had been a very long time coming. I had my granddaughter with me as her mom, my daughter, had to work. I remember my two sportsy sisters being very upset that she was along. Not showing any kindness to this kid or me, they talked openly about their disappointment. Jen decided she didn't have an important ingredient and she and Donna took off together to get it. The store was a good fifteen minutes away. My granddaughter and I tried to make the best of it, patiently waiting for their return and trying not to feel out of place, but we did.

Once back, they ganged up to scold me, again, in front of my sweet little granddaughter. We were not very far into the potica process when I decided to leave. I was so stunned and hurt and embarrassed to be crying in front of my granddaughter. We moved to leave. They started making fun of my hurt and tears. I did my best to stop crying, to soften it all on my way out but that was a stinker. I had come believing we were all adults now, and this kind of thing wouldn't happen anymore. Sadly, that kind of behavior was part of the training, the culture of being a jock. I was forty-five years old, Donna was forty-two and Jen, thirty-nine. I never did fit in with them, and now, looking back, I am grateful for that. My disappointment and sadness for that "family gathering" was too much for me to stay connected. Future events would, again, challenge that resolve.

III

I did get to watch and sometimes participate in a very limited way when my dad was fixing things. That was where my happiness landed. Fixing things, though it would not be an easily supported passion in this world dominated by male ego. There were times when I felt my dad's hate for my abilities to troubleshoot, to physically get my little hand in where his big hand failed, to loosen or tighten, hook up or take apart. I loved working with him, but he could not feel the same. That social brain wiring of insecurity ran too deep for us both. I had his brain for such things and his disdain for it also.

The only other place that seemed to let us spend time together was fishing. When my Aunt Flossy and Uncle Lorne had their cabin on Bassett Lake, we were often out in the motorboat, early in the morning, me stretching out too far toward the bow, always wanting my hands in the water and my face in the wind. He would remind me to stay seated securely by saying, "Sit down, god damnit!" I would be so rich if I had a dollar for every time he said "Can't you ever just sit still? What the hell is wrong you?"

I remember trying my best and still enjoying being out there with him. He could be very patient and kind, especially when I was quiet and happy just to be on the water, in the boat, with him. There were countless times that he had to re-worm or minnow my hook. There were times when my cast got stuck in his hat, or shirt sleeve or pant leg and sometimes even in his skin, but when I caught a fish, he was just as thrilled as if he had. And I got to help with the net when he had one on his fishing line. I loved being on, in, or near the water. I still do.

He taught me by letting me drive the boat, at first sitting on his lap or next to him, then on my own, as I grew. He taught all us kids how to operate and care for boats and outboard motors. Vent the gas tank, unlock to tilt the motor blades up and down, prime until the bulb is firm, throttle in neutral up about two thirds, choke it, start pulling the cord. Sometimes it took finessing between throttle and choke, but we all knew how to row our way back just in case. We learned to quickly adjust the tilt of the motor for moving over low water, lily pads, floating tree limbs, or rocks. How to pull out and in for docking and tie-up, and how to help put the boat in the boathouse. We also learned how to run the speed boat for water skiing and how to ski behind it.

My dad and I struggled so much. Trying to gain his love and approval was a lifelong quest. He was violent and angry with me most of my young life and even into my adulthood. After my mom and he got sober, it still wasn't great between us. We really had no understanding of one another though we both did our best in the later years, before he died. Here are some words about him, taken from his obituary:

> Tim grew up in Two Harbors, Minn., was drafted into the Navy in October of 1943 where he served with the 55th SeaBees Construction Battalion for twenty-two months and eight days. He spent the majority of his service in New Guinea and Australia.
>
> After he was discharged from the Navy, he settled back in Two Harbors, before attending the Milwaukee School of Engineering on the G.I. Bill. He was hired by IBM in 1947 and returned for additional schooling in Endicott New York. Tim retired from IBM in 1979, and started his own business selling small office equipment. He lived and raised his family in Hibbing, Minn., Pearl Harbor, Hawaii, and Duluth.

"Tim," as my dad was called, was called back to serve in the Korean War from 1950 to 1953 where he was stationed in Pearl Harbor. As far as I have been able to determine, he enlisted in the Navy for the first time on September 27, 1943. His duty was line-crew, installing and maintaining wiring for base living quarters and working in the armature shop primarily engaged in rewinding armatures and rebuilding or repairing electric motors. From there he enrolled in a two-year degree program at the Milwaukee School of Engineering (MSOE). Here's what Wikipedia says about this school:

> MSOE received the official seal of approval from the Society for the Promotion of Engineering in 1943, as part of recognition for educational achievements. The following year, MSOE also became a charter member of the National Council of Technical Schools. For the first time, the university started accepting females into its program in order to replace males who were drafted into World War II. Following the end of the war enrollment swelled in 1946 and 1947 due to the GI Bill of Rights allowing returning service personnel to pursue a college education. By 1947 over 90% of the students were veterans.

I cannot say with certainty, but it appears that he then went to a twenty-nine-week course in Endicott New York, to train to work for IBM as an accounting machine serviceman.

He went back into the Navy on July 7, 1950 on emergency naval duty assigned to CEP-Construction Battalion, Electrical Engineer and was shipped to, and lived on the islands of, the South Pacific. Tim was twice honorably discharged from naval duty, this time on the 2nd of October of the year 1953. That was four years before I was born. Tim (Walter Wright, Jr.) died at age eighty-eight in 2014.

IV

Wakefield, Michigan. The home of my paternal grandmother, Modesta Catherine, and my Great Uncle Roman who, unknown by me for many years, was the town drunk. Getting drunk feels at first like a good way to get demons out of one's mind, but the physical toll it takes on the body and brain and follows with the crooked forming of the sensitive heart and soul are much too devastating for all involved to make it a useful tool in life. I remember him caring for his dying wife, in a medical bed in the dining room of that house in Wakefield. I am now wondering if it may actually have been owned by Roman and his wife and my grandmother was the live-in family member, perhaps helping to care for her dying sister-in-law.

Uncle Ro, Uncle Ben and Uncle Ed, Modesta Catherine's brothers, were funny and kind and they loved us and enjoyed us for a day or two. When we stayed longer, they became annoyed, but never cruel. I had wonderful, beautiful, and fun cousins that lived in Babbit, Minnesota but often visited Wakefield at the same time we did. Staying with their grandmother, my Aunty Anne, Uncle Ed's wife, they lived about six blocks away, down the sidewalk that ran in front of my grandma's house and then a right turn and three houses on the right. Their son, my dad's cousin Shoodoo, (completely unsure of how that was spelled), was my dad's other drinking pal. My mom, Betty Lois and my Uncle Shoodoo's wife, Aunty Marlys, also enjoyed their cocktails together while all the cousins did what we could to enjoy our time together in Wakefield.

My grandmother's other brother, Uncle Ed, owned a tavern on the main street just a walk through the backyard of her house and through another yard or two. That place was dark in so many ways. It was there, just those few backyards from my grandmother's nurturing home, I was made to sit on the laps of drunk men. I was too little and powerless to even recognize how demeaning and demoralizing that experience was. Their joy of the moment overrode my horror and fear. I had no self. It was all about pleasing others, longing to be seen and loved as one little girl should be. This was not a good plan for teaching me to be wise and fully awake, and alive in my own body. I was completely void of knowing I had the option to say no, or to run away, out of the tavern door, into the sunshine.

The imprinted messages of the callous signs and bar trinkets showed women as shadows with boobs or just as boobs. That was all there was, breasts everywhere. And dirty sex memos. No heart or mind, no respectful feelings, no strength, or courage attached to them. No right to object, no way to say no, no voice to express how that damaged us all, male and female, young and old. But the women sat and drank with the men surrounded by these messages. I learned to disconnect every part of me from me. My brain was mapped to be used by whoever was in power.

V

My mom had some fairly violent and angry moments. Many as a matter of fact. She was physically corrected and punished as a child by so many, and she was also married to a violent alcoholic. One who was also very reliable, hardworking, funny at times and would fix and re-fix anything that got broken. He brought in a good income, shoveled the snow, fixed the cars, took us fishing, and I could go on. He did his best to provide. I've come to learn that he never wanted a big family, but he did his best. We were Catholic.

In 1960 the first oral contraceptive, Enovid, was approved by the US Food and Drug Administration (FDA) as contraception. In 1965, The Supreme Court (in Griswold v. Connecticut) gave married couples the right to use birth control, ruling that it was protected in the Constitution as a right to privacy.

Source: Boston Women's Health Book Collective. 1973. A brief history of birth control in the U.S. In: Our Bodies, Ourselves. Simon & Schuster.

I know my dad was pretty pleased to finally get a son after fathering six daughters, one of whom died shortly after birth. He had four daughters and then, finally, a son to pass along his funny name, neither of whom used it on an informal basis. There was my dad, Tim and my brother, Buddy. Now we call him Bud. Walter Rellis Wright Jr. and III.

My Aunt Flossy (my mom's sister) was the kindest, softest spoken and loving woman I've ever known. I know I couldn't see everything clearly as a child, but I know she loved and pampered us, all of us, my mom included. My dad and Flossy's husband, my Uncle Lorne seemed to have gotten along pretty well, fishing and boating, boat houses and cabins. Flossy didn't have any children of her own. I think she was unable, or Lorne was.

VI

It was Friday, June 24th 1976. I was in my sixth month of pregnancy and visiting my mom's house on Pitt Street. I remember standing in the living room, next to the front entryway as Flossy and Lorn came into the house with some very difficult news. My mom had been worried and talking about some of the troubles Flossy was having with her health. Flossy had just come from the doctor's office in Duluth and was crying and red faced as she shook her head from side to side in a "no" action telling my mom, "It's not good. I have Leukemia." And they hugged and cried. I don't think I knew what that was or how serious it was right then. I just couldn't imagine my aunt not being okay.

My mother had just accepted a job offer to take over for the night nurse that was retiring after many years of caring for the eighty-three-year-old heiress, Elisabeth Congdon. Betty would be working the night shifts in the huge old Glensheen Mansion on London Road starting that Sunday night. She felt bad about calling in to delay her start date but needed to be with her sister right now. We all went to the cabin at Bassett Lake on Saturday and stayed for two nights. On our drive home on Monday, as I sat in the middle of the back seat, I remember looking at the old high school on the hill that my mom and dad had attended as teenagers. As kids, we were always glad to see that landmark, visible for at least two miles, letting us know we were halfway home.

I was looking at the school as we listened to the radio report about the terrible murder that occurred the night before, at the Congdon Mansion. That was the night my mother was supposed to have started her new position as the night nurse. They had called the old nurse in for just one or two more nights, to cover.

My mother, Betty Lois, would have been murdered, though we, in order to better settle with this crazy occurrence, decided that Betty would have knocked the intruder over the head with something and saved the day. So it was that Flossy or Florence Lillian as she was named at birth, saved her little sister Betty Lois's life one last time.

My Auntie Flossy died on October 8th of 1977. I was only allowed to see her once, with her hair falling out in patches, and looking so sick. My daughter, Adeline Florence Jean was born eight days later.

VII

My parents almost always came and went through the back door. That is where the cars were parked. The back door faced west so a right turn was taken at the bottom of the stairs to head toward the garage. Attached to the garage by a clothesline, was a heavy metal T-bar that we also hung from by our knees and swung and jumped from, as often as we could, even onto the winter snow. Our garage sat with its front wall toward and about thirty feet from the back porch of our house, with its door facing the alley. I can still picture the gravel parking pad that Dad made for the other family vehicle, whatever it was at the time. It sat perpendicular to the garage and so parallel to the alley. My dad was quite the car buff, so we had many great vehicles as we were growing up, one house from the corner of 45th and Pitt St.

I remember some of his cars, but there were more. A white Dodge Lancer, a 1966 Studebaker that was red and cream or maybe it was blue, I get them mixed up in my head now. He had a big old white or silver Cadillac with long fins, and he owned an old round green Pontiac. I think that was the car my mom was driving when her foot slipped off the brake pedal and she rear-ended another car. I was pretty small, but I remember violently sliding off the front seat and down onto the floor as it happened. I wasn't hurt and neither was she but I remember sensing fear and trauma, and her guilt and shame, especially about reporting this to my dad. The training was clear, he was allowed to mess up, but the rest of us were not. His blame and rage were felt deeply and often.

Suddenly I am recalling another backdoor story. I have many flashbacks of years of joys and sorrows, pleasures and pains. Now here is this one coming back. I had been cleaning for many hours, vacuuming, and dusting, six baskets of clothes folded and put away and then vacuuming so there'd be a nice clean hallway at the top of the stairs. I made my parents' bed, cleaned the bathroom from top to bottom, the dining room and the living room all while being in charge of my younger sister and brother, getting them to bed, while my parents were out for the evening. The kitchen was a mess when they left, with food to be put away and many dishes to rinse and put in the dishwasher or wash, dry and put away. It seemed every pot and pan was dirty.

My dad had a strict rule that we all followed to a T with my one exception on this one night. The kitchen was my last room to clean before they came home. Dad's rule did not allow us to put any pots and pans in the dishwasher. By the time I got to the kitchen it was nearly 9:00 and I was tired and running out of time. I put the last pot in the dishwasher and ran it.

As it ran, I wiped off the table, the chairs, the stove top and burners, vacuumed and mopped the floor and wiped down the countertops and the refrigerator. Everything sparkled all over the house. Even the butler's pantry counter was neat and clean.

I was now the oldest child living at home, so I had a room of my own. It was the smallest bedroom and was at the top and to the left of the stairs. My door was just past the six feet of carpeted area, where floor meets wall, where we stored the clean clothes baskets until they could be put away. Often, in the rush of the morning's getting dressed for church or school, those baskets were dug through, so often clothes were in need of being refolded for putting in drawers or closets.

From the top of those stairs, which had a left turning curve, to the long stretch of sturdy carpeted steps, we could slide down on our bottoms, swiftly and smoothly landing on the widened, but only to the left, two bottom stairs. We kids all did this from the time we moved to this house until we got too big to not feel the pain in our backsides from it. I was just turning three when we moved in and I remember us discovering that if we lay on the floor and looked through the fat white ropes that were strung around the stairwell to keep us from falling through, we could see a little bit of the living room and the entire lower hallway which was the path to our grand front entry foyer and huge oak front door. We often lay there on our bellies, in the dark, listening to the adults as they came in to drink and party or drink and play bridge, remove their coats and place them in the closet to the left of the stairs.

This same stairwell was also good for climbing around on, to see if one or more of us could get all the way from the top of the stairs to the farthest wall without falling. We really were like a bunch of monkeys, always finding ways to climb on or swing from whatever might not break. As we each got tall enough, we would reach or jump ourselves up and forward, from one of the middle steps and grab the ropes, each hand grasping the two in the center, where they were attached to the hardwood framing by a metal eye-fastener. We would then swing back and forth for as long as possible and try to time it just right to swing out and down past the bottom stair to the main floor. Oh, how many times we didn't quite make it. I don't believe any of us was ever seriously injured by that type of play. We did pull the fasteners out from time to time. Our dad would grumble a bit and fix it.

But back to that night. After all my hard work, at about ten-fifteen, I was finally feeling like I'd done all I could to please my parents who were sure to be drunk when they came home, but happy with how clean the house was, and how much I'd accomplished. Surely they would be.

I was just starting to empty the dishwasher as my parents came through the back door earlier than expected. The dishwasher was to the left, as you walk through the very small vestibule to the kitchen. I was just reaching for that pot when he came around the corner and saw it in the rack. Instantly full of rage, he started screaming at me, and hitting me on the head. I was a teenager then, maybe fourteen or fifteen.

As I turned to run, one of his blows slammed me so hard that my head and body flew into the big refrigerator door. I hit it so hard it knocked me backward again toward him as I worked hard not to crumple but to run instead. I remember thinking "All that work I did, all that love and attention to the household and I'm getting this?" I scrambled with all my might to get up and out of the kitchen while he hit and slapped, and knocked me off my feet again, as I tried to run up the stairs. Besides the physical blows, he was reminding me of what a goddamn, no-good kid I was. He pulled me back by one foot as he ripped it out from under me. I had no way to flee. My mom was screaming at him to stop, and I think she finally pulled him off me. Then he went after her. I kept running to hide, to save my own skin.

My sisters were there waiting at their bedroom door, past mine and the bathroom to the left, and straight on in I ran. They quietly closed the door as I sat on the bed and cried. My sisters started pushing the dresser in front of the door, but stopped when they heard the screams and cries coming from my mom. They went running, though quite cautiously over to the railing to try to see what was happening. My mother was wailing, and my dad was still bitching but was going out the back door. After they heard the door slam shut, my sisters ran down to find my mom crying and moaning in pain as she lay amid the broken marble coffee table we were all so proud to have in our living room. I was halfway down the stairs when my dad came running back in, realized the mess he had made, and started to help mom up as we all flinched away, my sisters to the couch, and I up a few of the stairs. She couldn't get up, she couldn't stand. She cried, saying she thought she had a broken hip.

I never did work as hard at pleasing my parents after that. I got into drinking and drugs with my friends. I tried to figure out how to be with boys, but I was empty of self so it never worked well. It would be many years before I started to heal and learn who I was and what I really wanted.

I WANT TO also let you know that he, my dad, Tim, could be very kind and loving, funny and playful, and he worked tirelessly to fix anything that we broke, including two ski-doos and later two moto ski snowmobiles that he would let my friends and me take off on when I was a teenager. He worked on getting us bicycles and ice skates, sports equipment for those that used and needed it, and supported and cheered us for anything that we reached for.

VIII

The children of John Otto and Mary Norgren lived their lives as best they could, some having children and continuing the trauma, as is the way we humans seem to do, at least some of us. When we are still too young to have the time and the tools, the understanding of ourselves and how our traumas affect us, we marry or we don't. Either way, when we have children, we cannot help but pass on the trauma, the anger, the shame, the guilt. Punishment and violence are hardwired into our brains. Though our hearts wish never to pass on these legacies, it happens to the best of us. Somewhere along the way, opportunities arise that will teach us how to look within, see ourselves, and finally face the inherited fear and loathing we find. That is where freedom started for me.

The catch or not catch, as I have come to understand, is that one must be able to feel in order to move into the healing part of this living. I know now that not all of us are able. Feeling is not easy. Some of us cannot help but feel it all, some of it gets stored, hidden in the mind only to come forth for inspection when it is time, perhaps when we are ready. But I did not feel ready for most of my upheavals. I had no choice but to allow and feel them and I am grateful to have had the tools and the courage to allow them to move me. I had the opportunity to learn how to investigate, and then to work to understand how to head into, and heal me, one little bit at a time. This has been the most important part of my life story and I would never have been so open to it without my mom and my dad first taking that same courageous leap into mental and emotional healing and health.

Betty Lois went to treatment for alcoholism somewhere near the end of my sixteenth year. My dad followed and got sober six months later. They both attended AA and my mom started attending Al Anon meetings. They tried to get us all involved but, at that time, I was certainly not interested in the new and improved parenting they were offering. They sponsored and helped many people in their steady use of, and continued practice of, the twelve steps of both AA and Al Anon.

It took me until I was in my early thirties before I realized I too was not emotionally healthy. I started to see a wonderful therapist, Yvonne Prettner Solon, and she convinced me to try Al-anon. I started attending meetings in the Lester Park neighborhood and was determined that I would get through all twelve steps in one year's time. It's okay to have goals. After eleven years, I was finally getting through my twelfth step. It changed me for the better and for life.

I was barely nineteen when I got pregnant, not married and had no intention of marrying the man that I had been dating for about a year. I became a single parent. My daughter was just ten years old when her beloved grandmother, Betty Lois, started losing her mind.

I had some amazing and poignant moments in the six years that my dad and I, and sometimes others in the family, took care of and kept my mom safe while she diminished right before our eyes.

Six years after mom's diagnosis, on Christmas, we were at the same sister's house for our family Christmas Eve dinner and gifts gathering. This time, my first ever fiancé was with us. I was thirty-six years old and never married. My daughter was now sixteen. During our family dinner at a lovely big table of family and food, we must have discussed our wedding because what happened after dinner stunned us all.

My mom had no ability to understand or participate in my excitement about my wedding. She was just no longer there. That was a heartbreaker for me. She had supported me in every way while

I worked at being a single mom, being gainfully employed, and buying a house and paying the bills. She always wished for me to find a partner, but I was not willing to chance living with or marrying any of the men I had dated, which really didn't happen often. It was just too hard and I knew I was tough to match.

So on this Christmas Eve we finished our meal and went to the living room to open presents. When done, I asked my mom if she would like to have a cup of eggnog with me. She and I went to the kitchen, where my youngest sister stood talking to my other sister whose home we were visiting, and who was finishing up the dinner dishes. As I handed my mom her little cup of eggnog, she stopped me before I could sip saying "Oh no, wait, I'd like to make a toast." I looked at her in shock and lifted my cup to meet hers. "Here is to your wedding," and we clinked. "Didn't think I knew, did you?" And then she repeated that lovely phrase I remembered so well, "Have a beauty day." As we sipped she was gone again. I answered that I didn't think she knew. Her response was "Knew what?" She was gone.

I looked to my right and my youngest sister's mouth was open in shock. I think mine was too. No one would have believed me if it had just been the two of us. We all had a heck of a time with that one. I was so thrilled that somehow she knew and could be happy about it with me for a moment or two, but the heartache for me was wondering if she was still in there somewhere, perhaps stuck in a body and mind that held her prisoner.

As I write this to you, I am sixty-two years old and having some brain issues of my own. Not the same mechanism as my mom, but some kind of episodes that come up about once a month for two to three days. I can feel it coming on for at least a minute or two and then I lose full consciousness, though not completely going into what feels like a tunnel in my head. They vary so much in intensity and usually by the second day have gotten much lighter and more bearable. Also, they are overall, much less intense than they were during the first six months. At one point, while in the emergency room, my heart rate went down to thirty beats per minute. It has become pretty clear that my heart is not the problem. These episodes seem to be affecting my memory, though I come back pretty quickly and with some heavily concentrated effort I can find my way back to whatever I was doing in my pretty complex and busy job. It seems to be diminishing in intensity and perhaps in number. I am hoping that it will eventually go away. My daughter and I are holding out for the best and seeking answers, though so far it doesn't seem likely that it will be definitive.

Much evidence is showing that an abusive childhood could very well have created my brain issues. Please, please don't hit, or berate children. It is not useful and does much more harm than you can see in their young little eyes. They are unable to express how hurt and derailed they are. Their brains are not formed enough, that is the normal state and medically factual as far as can be determined now. Many proven studies have shown the development of the brain and how it forms beliefs about self and others, and forms habits to survive. Thriving can be totally put aside until all the negative brain paths can be rewired by truth and self and other nurturing. Critical data to learn who we are is presented by our parents, our siblings, our teachers, clergy, television, and music. Certain areas of the brain do not fully develop early in life, and some not until after the teens. They really cannot discern, work out or understand what their parents often punish them for. That part of the brain is still in the process of being created.

How horribly detrimental to their sense of self, to have no way to know what is wrong with them when their parents don't understand the truth about a developing mind and body. Positive, they say. Give them ways to practice and learn that is based in positivity. They will fall down and get back up many times in life. They need to hear from you that this is perfectly healthy and normal, that they are okay, no matter what has just occurred. Teach them again and again, give them tools to use when they are unsure, that will feed their self-esteem and curiosity. Find ways to redirect when you are worn out by being the director parent and take breaks. Do them no harm and you will never regret it. Apologize when you have, and then you teach them to be okay with making mistakes and apologizing. Have no regrets, just start from now. They, and you will benefit quickly and thoroughly.

There were many threats of being sent to Moose Lake when we were not behaving as my mom would like us to. I'm betting she too was severely threatened with joining her biological mother in the nut-farm.

Part 6
Betty's Decline and Death

I

For Christmas of 1987, since my sister Donna, two- and one-half years younger than I, had the biggest house and family, we were all invited to her house for our family Christmas Eve tradition. I think this was also the first year we drew straws for exchanging gifts. We were a bigger family now, with grandchildren, spouses and such, so exchanging gifts between every one of us was just not wise. I drew my mom's name. When I asked her what she wanted, she said a great pair of tennis shoes for her annual trip to Florida with my dad. They had bought a trailer home in a retirement community in Tavares. They always left the great north woods after the holidays and stayed away for three months. So she and I went shopping. We found the perfect pair at Haddad Shoes on East 4th Street. I took them home and wrapped them up. We agreed that she would pretend to be delighted and surprised.

My sister Jen, six years younger than I and my brother Buddy, who was ten years younger than I, still lived with Mom and Dad, but on Gilliat Street now. They had sold the bigger Pitt Street house sometime after I had moved out at age eighteen. My brother could be very cruel and cutting to and about my mom, and often told her, and anyone that would listen, that she was nuts, that she was losing her mind. I really hated all that and tried to stay away as much as I could, though I had a new baby girl and she and my mom adored each other. The family history of mental illness was not to be played with, like I felt my brother was doing. He was disconnected from any sort of sensitive truths, as he was trained to be, by my dad and society. It was years of brother Bud moving in and out I think. My memory is very unclear on this.

No matter which of us showed up at our Pitt Street house, my mom always offered a meal, and loving hugs, good conversation and any help she was able to provide, to all of us. She was a sincerely good and loving human being. She was a good mom, and improved with her sobriety and age. She learned how to guide and help others unconditionally, with a full and generous heart. No matter where she was and which one of us was with her, we all realized how many people loved and admired her, and how many she had sponsored or helped in other ways. She would, so many times during an outing, stop to say hello, and often hug people, always remembering their names. "Have a beauty day!"

Our family tradition was to eat our Christmas Eve meal, which we did mid-afternoon, clean up the kitchen, and then all sit in a circle in the living room and the kids would pass out gifts, one at a time. We all watched while my mom opened her gift from me. She took one shoe out, looked at it like she had never seen it before as I sat across the room feeling very impressed by her show of not knowing. She then asked in a very angry voice "Who got me these?" while very sincerely looking around the room at all of us. "These will never fit me, and they certainly aren't anything that I would pick out." My head was very confused. It didn't take too long for me to realize that she wasn't acting surprised, she was sincerely surprised and truly upset which was not her nature in such a situation. My heart sank. She didn't remember shopping for them with me. I asked her that question and she verified her stance. Everyone in the room was confused. The larger concerns came later but that was the beginning of the end of my having a mom.

I hated it that Bud had been seeing things for at least a year before the shoe incident and that we all ignored him. He had been saying she was losing it since he was thirteen. Without being given a kind and compassionate way of voicing his experiences, we all just thought it was just his age and his demeanor. How sad to not be heard, while watching your mom fail mentally.

II

For six years I watched and waited for Mom to die. I was tired. Tired of wondering how this would end. Tired of feeling bad about wanting it to. I think I asked her heart to give up a dozen or two times. She was no longer with us.

I sat with her trying to stop her as she repeatedly tried to rip the oxygen hose out of her nose, and take all of the medically connected devices off so she could go home. We were in the ICU. She would look at me, as I sat nearly on her, and say, "Why are you keeping me here? I'm going home," and try to raise her arms to get her hands to her face to do damage to herself and equipment. I would try to calm her again, by telling her the truth, or a story, or anything to get her to sit still. We did this life or death dance for hours until she slapped me. I called the nurses in to let them know I couldn't do this anymore. They gave her a shot to put her to sleep. I tried to rest but instead, would listen to each breath, to each beep of the heart monitor, wishing it would just all stop. I was literally asking each breath to please, please be the last one. I sat there longing for her to die and hating myself for it. Wrestling with it all instead of resting.

We took her home again.

One of my very first jobs had been at Lakeshore Lutheran Nursing home. My mom and I worked in the laundry room, washing and drying, mangling and folding, bag after bag of laundry. I worked in the kitchen doing dishes for a while too. One hot sweaty day down in the basement with her, as we pushed and pulled wet laundry around, she made me promise her that I would never put her in a place like this. I was more than willing to agree to that. I promised her that I would not.

I had to push my dad to put her in that same nursing home for his sanity and her safety. She had started a fire at home. She could not stop moving. My dad couldn't get any sleep. She was now quite a danger to them both.

I was arm and arm with her as we walked her in. She was so far gone I knew she wouldn't have any way to realize how bad this felt. My dad had done an amazing job for six years. I never would have guessed how devoted and attentive he would be with her. A very dear friend of both my mom and dad was so good to help him through this. My dad's IBM co-worker suffered from dementia for twelve years. His wife, Dee Dee, took care of him. He died a few years before my mom got sick, I think. She was amazingly helpful to Dad and all of us, as we tried to do our best.

Dad and Dee Dee became best friends. Some of my family members were not pleased by this but I was. They never did anything to hurt my mom, just the opposite, from my perspective. I was the closest one to the fire with my dad. He did a good job loving them both with his whole heart.

Once we got to Mom's room at the nursing home, we were accompanied by two of the staff members. I was still arm-in-arm with her. She looked around and asked what we were doing here? "I don't really need to visit here right now." she said. "Let's go home." My breath started to shorten. I decided to bring her to the window to show her what a nice view we had. She saw the blue fake vinyl chair with blond wooden arms and legs and sat down very angrily. She grabbed the arms of the chair and looked right at me. "You promised me you would never do this! You cannot leave me here!" She didn't shout but she was firm, clear and angry.

I had no words. I couldn't breathe. I went out to the well-lit hallway and cried and cried. I couldn't stop. I fell to the floor, sliding my left side down the wall. How was I ever going to be able to leave her here?

III

I am so hesitant to tell you this next part as it really did baffle me, and I am sure some of you won't believe that it occurred, but if you knew me, you would know I am not one to fabricate. It took me a year to finally see a psychologist about this occurrence.

I owned a little house on Dodge Street in the far east side of the Lakeside neighborhood of Duluth. My daughter and I lived pretty well there, though I didn't have neighbors that I felt close to, as they were mostly middle aged to older folks with no children at home. No other single parents nearby for support. There weren't very many of us at that time in the world.

My habit, when I was not working a night shift, was to read for at least half an hour before turning out the lights to sleep. It was one of those nights and all seemed normal until I closed my eyes. From the instant that I did, I was suddenly struggling to breathe. My awareness was very strange as I tried to reason this out. The conversation with myself was one of questioning why it should come on so suddenly. I was fine just moments ago. How could it change like that? What was going on and what should I do? This went on for about ten minutes, and then the phone, next to my bed, rang.

I put the phone to my ear and said "hello" with much concern, while tossing the covers aside, sitting myself up on the side of the bed and putting my feet on the floor. It was my dad's voice. "Cathy!" he said so seriously. "Would you please come to the hospital?" I looked at the clock. It was nearly midnight. My dad went on: "Honey, it's your mother. She's having some kind of asthma attack and we cannot get her breathing under control. Can you please come down and see if you can help her? It's just horrible!" he said, and again with such heartbreak "It's just horrible."

"Yes, of course." I said, looking at the clock again. "Which hospital?" I hung up the phone and felt so unsure about what I was feeling. I was quite aware that I was no longer having any trouble breathing which was really messing with my head. I got dressed wondering about my mom and my strange experience with my horrible chest congestion as I fell asleep. Did I just dream it?

I don't remember the drive to the hospital or walking in, I just remember getting into the Emergency Room and seeing her struggle with her breath, sitting upright and moving around like she was on fire. In the past, I had been very good at calming my grandmother down when she was starting to fail, having trouble breathing. Experiencing her response to my loving attention, I decided it was my grandmother's fear and anxiety causing her short and labored breaths. For my grandmother, just sitting on the side of her bed and gently touching her chest in a circular motion, with my eyes on hers, and my face near hers worked beautifully. As I talked to her and soothed with my touch her breathing slowed back to normal.

For my mother, it became quickly apparent that nothing I tried to do had any effect. It was horrible to watch; she was writhing and struggling, while begging us all to help her. I cannot remember the rest of that night.

I think it was the next day that we were told that Mom's heart was only working at sixteen percent of what it should be. Her entire heart was hardening. Not just one or two of the quadrants, which is more usual. It was her entire heart. The physicians were surprised that she did as well as she did and they explained why hat is probably why she cannot sit still. She needed to move to keep her blood flowing. My heart felt broken and stunned, but part of me was grateful that something was going to keep her from living with this dementia for too many more years for any of us to endure and manage.

Author's note: I wrote this after that diagnosis.

They say your heart is hardening,
I know that's just not true.
The hugs you give me tell me
there's still lots of love in you.

Your memory is failing,
But your nature stays so warm,
Your gentle caring way still shines,
Your humor, still a charm.

I know that you'll be leaving soon.
I've missed you now, three years.
I look at you and wonder if
Inside you share my tears.

So hard to watch you slip away,
The slowness is unkind.
The one thing I hold onto is that
somewhere in your mind
You see how much like you I am,
How much will stay behind.

I thank you for these gifts you gave me,
Know this as you go.
I'll carry on the love you felt,
I'll let your spirit show.

IV

It was not just her breathing symptoms that I could feel. At least that was just in my sleep so far. She felt like she had to pee constantly. Her body was not able to filter and take care of the liquids like it should. She used the bathroom thirty times a day. When we were out somewhere I had to take her to the bathroom so many times. I had to quit taking her places; it was just too difficult.

At this point, my dad had changed the locks on the side and front doors of their home to a key only, no knob to turn to lock or unlock, so that she could no longer leave without him knowing it. I was stunned when he called me very early one dark, cold morning, telling me that she was missing again. Stunned and really scared.

I started driving again in my part of the Lakeside, Lester Park neighborhood. Back and forth along Superior Street looking at all the gas stations, and any place I thought she may have stopped to wait for help or rest. It started getting lighter outside and as I passed the gas station that we all knew so well, one that my brother had worked at for years, I saw a man walking from the main door out to the gas pumps. We knew the owner and he knew all of us. I didn't recognize this man, but he seemed to know me. I really don't recall anything other than, after rolling down my window getting ready to ask him, he asked me if I was looking for a little gray-haired woman that seemed lost. I was thrilled to say "Yes!"

He went on to say "She was walking by and said she was lost. I told her I thought she knew the people that live in that yellow house." As he pointed to what I knew was Marge and Bruce Weatherby's home, across the railroad tracks about three hundred feet down the sidewalk. "She is there, safe and sound." he assured me. I thanked him and was knocking on the back door before I knew it. She was there, and my dad was on his way as they had already called him.

I told them about the man at the gas station. They said that the station shouldn't have anyone there at this time of morning. It was barely 6:00 a.m. Bob doesn't get there until 7:30 to open. I described him, but no one could ever figure out who it was that directed my mom to the Weatherby's and me to my mom. Not Bob, the owner, either. He said there would be no way someone else was in this station at that time of the morning.

My dad and I pondered how she got out, but the key was near the door in case of emergency, he just didn't think she would figure it out. She did.

We never learned who that man was that sent her to safety and directed me to her.

V

At thirty years old and the single parent of a ten-year-old daughter, working full time and on rotating twelve-hour shifts at the Lake Superior Paper Mill, it was now my other job to help my dad take care of my mom. My two other sisters couldn't help much. Jen lived fifteen minutes out of town and had a very demanding job with the St. Louis County Court System as a social worker for kids that had gotten in trouble with the law. Donna lived about ten minutes away, but she had four boys to raise and also a demanding job as a teacher in the Duluth Public School System and a husband to do battle with.

Neither Jen nor I were married, though Jen did have some pretty significant relationships. None of us did very well choosing our mates. Right or wrong, Donna was the only one of us females that stuck with the one she started with. My sisters were both wonderful at their work and were very much needed. My brother was neither in the right frame of mind nor available. He had joined the military and it took him into some pretty amazing places where he found his wife and life partner in Honduras. Then into some horribly difficult war experiences that further chewed him up and left him even more scared than my dad had been.

It wasn't long after our Christmas Day jolt of Mom not being okay, that my dad took her to the doctor's office and they diagnosed dementia by scanning her brain. It was progressive and things got very strange and difficult. She recognized me throughout, and that was a blessing. We recognized pretty quickly that she became less and less able to sit still. My dad reported that she would strip their bed, wash and dry the linens, call him to help her make the bed again and a little while later, strip the bed again and be washing the same linens before he realized what she was doing.

She washed dishes, took things out of the drawers all over the house and put them back in and she would go for walks. That didn't seem to be a problem until one day, my dad called me and wondered if Mom was still at my house. I said she never was. We both went in search. I started out in my neighborhood, further east than their home, driving around, stopping to ask if anyone had seen a spunky little white-haired woman walking by. I think I was out for about fifteen or twenty minutes. We didn't have cell phones then. I drove up 54th Avenue East and when I approached the old library, which had been closed for a couple years, I saw carpenters' trucks on the street side of the building. Something told me to go check it out. I was just getting up to the door and out she came. She was happy to see me, telling me that she couldn't find my house. "I couldn't remember where you lived," she said. "I recognized this building so

I went in to see if I could use the bathroom. The people inside were very kind."

I took her back to her house and waited for my dad to come back. We decided to be sure to call each other as she was leaving from now on, so I could be aware and watch for her, or just go get her and not let her walk to my house anymore. Looking back, we certainly did not have enough understanding or information about this kind of disease.

I would go get her as often as I could and take her with me running errands or just to the mall to walk. She really just couldn't sit still very well. It was quite an experience, as her brain died off in what seemed like layers, she would talk of things I had never heard before. She started to sing a very old and strangely tempoed song, in another language. It had to have been either Swedish or Finnish as those were my adoptive grandparents' origins and it was one of their parents or relatives that she learned it from. I worked hard to learn it as she sang it and finally got it. We would sing it while I drove us to wherever we were going next. That was such a joy for us both. I can't remember how long that lasted but once it faded for her, it faded for me.

It was a grueling six years of trying to do it all well, and stay sane. I was a wreck and not the best parent. I got Lyme disease, but it wasn't diagnosed properly. They told me I was borderline positive for Lupus Erythematosus. My body was failing me terribly and I needed to keep working at the papermill. The shift work was making it impossible, and my daughter started into some very deep psychological trouble so I begged my employer to be given an office position and promised to learn it well and be useful.

They gave me an office job but cut my income by ten thousand per year. I was terrified to lose the little house I'd bought and struggled to take care of everything and all of us. I had to find a way to make enough money. The papermill started harassing me about some really inane things and started some very harsh actions against me, beating me up in a large meeting once a month for six months. They never took into account what I was dealing with. It was one of the worst employment situations I'd ever been through.

When I started there, they wouldn't hire me as a shift electrician, which is what I had been working as prior at the papermill in Two Harbors, because I was a woman. A friend of mine, who worked as a counselor in the offices of the Lake Superior Paper Company, came to tell me that. She said if they did agree to hire me on a trial basis, I would have to be paid less than the guys, because I wasn't coming off the production floor but from an office job. I told her she better check the law. She had a degree in human resources. They wouldn't consider me for that Electrical Department until after I'd been working there for a year. Once my year was up, after being an excellent employee, they still wouldn't, when an opening came up.

They worked against me for years, monetarily and emotionally, very publicly beating me, all while I was trying to learn to be, and succeeded in becoming, a very good office worker, doing much of the billing and buying for all the chemicals and products needed to make and ship the paper we were making, creating better ways to manage and document usage and costs.

VI

I went to see her every day, though my life really didn't allow for it, I did. At least for the first month. Each time I arrived, I would look in her room and see that she was not there and start walking the corridor that was a huge connected square walking path for her. I would walk and watch for either her back, as she walked her distinctive kicky walk, so full of vip and vinegar, or her coming toward me. That dancey little kick in her walk as if she were on cloud nine. If she was walking away from me all I had to do was call her name, "Betty!"

She would spin with glee and come literally dancing toward me with such a beautiful smile on her face. Once she got close enough, and it was always the same, she would hug me and hold me close while stating clearly and firmly, "Let's go get my coat. Get me out of here." And every time I would have to pull my heart back together and redirect the plan. There were times when I would take her for a ride but I never took her to my house or to hers. It would just be too hard to bring her back. My dad would come get her on his motorcycle, always bringing two helmets. She loved that.

At the nursing home, the locked ward had a button that was installed high up on the frame of the door, to push for those that should be coming and going. They had to have it moved up higher than she could reach, as she figured that one out very quickly. She was going home, that was all there was to it.

My dad and Dee Dee decided to go to Florida. I agreed to stay at my dad's house, with my daughter, taking care of their cat, and my mom at the nursing home, while they were away. I felt they really needed and deserved that break. I think they were planning on being gone for a few weeks.

Adeline and I had been staying there for about a week. I slept in my parents' room and Adeline slept in the bedroom at the top of the stairs. One night at around 2:00 a.m. the house phone rang. There were three extensions. As I answered and tried to wake myself enough to understand what was being said, the woman on the phone was telling me that she was calling from Lakeshore Lutheran Home to tell me that my mother had expired. "Expired?" I responded with anger and confusion. "Yes," she said. "I'm sorry to have to tell you...." And she said it the same way again. I was so angry. I think I asked her "What do you mean, expired?"

Suddenly I heard Adeline's sixteen-year-old voice saying, "Mom, Grandma Betty died." A moment of silence and then she said it again, "She is dead, Mom."

I woke up enough and it became clear. I asked what I needed to do next and the woman on the phone said "Someone from the family needs to come down to the home as soon as possible. We cannot move her until a family member has seen and identified the body." I don't remember the wording thereafter, but Adeline and I got dressed and drove the four blocks to Lakeshore.

That was January 11, 1993. I'll never forget my senses as I arrived in the room. From at least eight feet away, I knew what I was seeing was just her shell. She was gone. I was relieved. I had no connection to her dead body. Not a drop. I felt no sense of loss, only her freedom. Not even mine at that moment, just hers.

I stopped feeling like I had to pee every half hour, the intensity and pain of it gone. I was free from feeling her varying symptoms, but I wasn't totally free. A few weeks after her funeral, I had the strangest dream. The entire family was all hanging out in a huge, rounded section of a beautifully red bricked, underground tunnel. It was the sewer system and the water was coming and going in open troughs. Some of the water was flowing from outlets that were up higher than our heads, and some from down lower and the water was flowing so softly and sweetly.

I knew it was a sewer but it felt like a water feature at a park with very clean fresh water flowing through it. I was watching from afar somehow, like floating in the air. I could see my dad and my siblings moving around like it was no big deal. What bothered me was that my mother's body would suddenly be floating from one side of the cavern to the other to disappear again and no one did anything. My family just kept on with whatever they were doing, almost like they were having a picnic or something. Each time her body would appear, I called to them to do something, to go get her, to pull her out before she disappeared again. They would never heed my requests. It seemed they wouldn't or couldn't hear me. Sometimes she would be coming out of one of the upper trough outlets and her body would bend and float smoothly with the water that was carrying her from place to place, like she was made of paper or of liquid.

I felt terribly guilty for not doing something. I felt sad and angry at my family for just ignoring me and her. It's been twenty-seven years and I can still see it as if it is happening now. I don't think I'll ever understand or forget that dream.

Part 7
My Search: The Records

I

Eight Norgren siblings survived to adulthood. They are, in birth order, Deward, Vernon, John, Doris, Florence, Dougal, Albert, and Betty. Below is the information I found on them at the Minnesota Historical Society, with this exception: I included some information I found on Betty and on Florence in earlier chapters.

May 8, 1930. *Letter from Judge W. E. Scott, Judge of Probate, Lake County to the State Public School in Owatonna, Minnesota*

> Gentlemen:
> There is a case in Two Harbors in regard to which we want to ask your advice.
>
> There is a family here of eight children as follows:
> Deward Norgren---18 years
> Vernon Norgren   16 "
> John Norgren   15 "
> Doris Norgren   13 "
> Florence Norgren 11 "
> Dougal Norgren   9 "
> Betty Norgren   5 "
> Albert Norgren   6 "
>
>   The oldest boy, Deward, is taking care of himself and works at the Steel Plant at Duluth. The other seven children are attending the public schools here.
>   The mother of the children is at the State Hospital at Willmar and is unable to take care of them. The father of the children, namely John Otto Norgren, was killed in an automobile accident April 23, 1930.

Will you kindly advise us what should be done in a case like this? May the children be sent to the State school at Owatonna? If so, are they committed directly to your school and, if not committed, how should they be committed?

It appears that some of the children could be placed with families here in Two Harbors. In that event would the children still remain wards of the state?

As this is an urgent case, we would deeply appreciate a quick reply as well as any further information, including procedure, you may give us which will help us solve this problem to the best interest of the children.

    Yours very truly,
    W. E. Scott, Judge of Probate
    (Appendix O)

II

Deward Otto, my mother's oldest brother, first child of Mary McNeill and John Otto Norgren, was born on March 15, 1912. I knew his daughter, whom we all called Auntie Joan, fairly well. I've met his other daughter, Donna only a few times, but her smile and delicate form were important to me. They both gave me hope that our family had graceful and yet strong women, that goodness could come from tragedy and madness. My dad had told me once that Uncle Deward had horrible anger and rage in him and was described as having mental problems. I have no proof or clarity on that. I don't have any photographs of Deward.

Then Vernon. He was the one killed at or near the Battle of the Bulge. He was forty-three years older than I and he died at age thirty.

THOSE MENTIONED ABOVE were the three older boys that did not have to go to the orphanage. I had no idea about their lives, only that they were grown up and had children or went to war and died. My mother always spoke of it all with so little regret or emotion. She may have felt much, but didn't show it or share it with me. Perhaps she learned to turn it off, put it away, not feel. I wish I could ask her all my questions. I wish I could have been a bit older and wiser before she started fading away. I could have asked her when I was ready. We could have talked. I might have understood so much more.

She was the youngest at less than two years old when her mother was taken away. They all learned to keep the worst of it to themselves. The stories I have, firsthand from my mother, were short versions of what she did remember or what she was told by her siblings when they talked about it.

Neither Deward, Vernon nor John was taken to the orphanage. The information I can find about their lives after their father died is hard to come by. The children were well trained in not talking about any of this very painful time for all involved.

Deward was eighteen, Vernon was sixteen and John was only fourteen years old when their younger siblings were taken away to the orphanage. Deward married Marie. I met them as a married couple many times as they grew old together.

There is evidence they were together by December 24, 1931 from a note showing they sent a gift of modeling clay to the orphanage for Albert at Christmas. That is one year and seven months from the time the children were taken to the orphanage. Deward was twenty years old when he sent a gift to his sister Doris at the orphanage. I can see that Deward had a job. John Wendell was taken in by, and helped take care of, his grandmother Betty, John Otto's mother.

I don't remember hearing much about Vernon, though my mom did speak of him. I do know that Vernon went to war at age thirty, and died near the Battle of the Bulge that year. I have not learned if he was married. I don't remember being told of any cousins.

Here is a letter he wrote to Doris from Somewhere in Europe:

Nov. 12, 1944
Somewhere in Europe
Dear Doris:

Received your welcome letter and was glad to hear that things are not too bad. Marie had said that Dougal would be home but he never writes. I did finally hear from Albert. It's tough here and we have to be rugged but I am still well and all in one piece. We've seen about three months of action - more than I bargained for. We still hope to get it over with before to long.

We've watched the bombers come and go and the buzz bombers come but don't know where they are going. It's quite a contraption.

It's damp and cold now and the outlook not to good for a comfortable winter. I dread these long dark nights very much. Not the best way to enjoy life after thirty but I think we're putting the finish on Hitler's outfit so it's not in vain.

There's not too much to write about and stay in our limits. The people here are very industrious and not to bad off although they do not have to much of things. It's not as bad as one might expect.

Their towns are modern and most living places not to bad, in fact I would (not) mind owning some of these quaint little places with their thatched roofs. The farms are kind of built around a court or square and the home and barn and livestock with feed just go around and around and some times over lap. There's plenty of noise to lull one to sleep. Sheep, pigs, chickens, horses, cattle, cats and dogs and hay to sleep on. We get to use the barns once in a while and have used up a lot of these farmers hay. That's a cheap price to pay I think although some of them give us the eye. All told they're glad to help along.

One might learn to like it here if they never lived in the good old United States.

I'll have to sign off now and see how the guard is set up. Pleasant dreams and seasons greetings if I don't get around to it. Greet the old man when you write my greeting to everyone.

Love, Vernon (Appendix P)

The Battle of the Bulge was fought from December 16, 1944 to January 16, 1945 and was also known as the Ardennes Offensive. It was the largest battle fought on the Western Front in Europe during World War II.

Pfc. Vernon B. Norgren
Company A
Died January 22, 1945 1/2 mile S of Born Belgium
MOS: unknown
Home State: MN & IL
Buried at Lakeview Cemetery; Two Harbors, MN

I found the following on the internet:
Vernon B. Norgren
Author: wwjohnston
Date: Saturday, February 19, 2011
Surnames: Norgren, Sandwick
Vernon B Norgren was a member of Company A, 17th Tank Battalion, 7th Armored Division, when his tank was hit by artillery 1/2 mile south of Born, Belgium, 22 Jan 1945, killing him and three others in the crew.

Vernon is listed on the web page of 17th Tank Battalion WWII dead. His dog tag listed his next of kin as Deward Norgren of Duluth, Minnesota. However his next of kin on his records was his step-father John W. Sandwick of Knife River, Minnesota (beneficiaries were his step-father and step-mother Gertie Sandwick). Mrs. John Sandwick was the housekeeper so she and her husband must have taken Vernon in as their step-son. This is totally new information for me, as I have no memory of my mother, or anyone, talking about the Sandwicks in any conversation or story.

Vernon Basil Norgren is buried at Lakeview Cemetery in Two Harbors, Minnesota. However despite the multiple Minnesota connections, he was apparently living in Rockford, Illinois when he was drafted, since the Army records give his home address as such.

III

Doris Marian, the first female child born to Grandmother Mary McNeill, was born December 7, 1916. My only memory of my Auntie Doris is of darkness, and pain. I think I may have met her once in person and realized how crippled, pale and weak she looked. She was red-haired and fair-skinned. I also remember a time when I was taken to her house out in West Duluth, I have no idea how old I was, maybe eight? Or twelve? I did not see her at all that day.

My memory is of being told, as I stood in that house, wishing with all my heart that I could run out, that she was bedridden upstairs, suffering from crippling arthritis. I remember that her daughters were red-headed and pale-skinned with beautiful lips and incredible eyes and hair. I remember liking them and their smiling playfulness. I remember my cousin Jeannie the most. She's now passed on. Her sister and I almost met in Minneapolis, to research and share at the Minnesota History Center, but she changed her mind. We did meet for lunch in Duluth but she wasn't terribly comfortable talking about the past. Our past is painful, and some of it so horrid to learn about after all the first victims are dead and gone.

IN A LETTER written on June 21, 1930 to the Judge of Probate in Two Harbors, Mr. Jager, State Agent in Owatonna also reported that he found that Mrs. Olson had changed her mind about taking Doris and that he thought it wise that she do so. It seems they had discovered that Doris has a slight curvature of the spine and also a positive tuberculin test. He adds that this, of course, makes it unwise to send her to a home until everything has been done to correct her defects. Besides, she objects to going to Mrs. Olson's home as she does not like the young man in the family.

(*Author's note: I am still unsure about which Mrs. Olson this was.*)

THE LINE IN the above letter that broke my heart a bit more is the one that tells of Mrs. Olson changing her mind about taking Doris because of the finding of the curvature of her spine and also a positive tuberculin test. My Aunty Doris had it so bad, and from what I remember of her, she was the most frail and the least able to defend or take care of herself. I know she married and had children, two wonderful girls, whom I have had the pleasure of knowing. I hope she was able to find joy and comfort within that family experience.

My great grandmother Betty, the mother of John Otto Norgren, worked hard to get custody of Doris. She applied for custody on April 25th of 1933. She wrote to Doris four months after they were sent to the orphanage, though she may have written sooner, I don't have all the documentation. Great-grandma Betty lived close to the

Knife River area, right on the shore of Lake Superior. Her home had been on the lake side of the North Shore drive but was damaged at some point and moved to the other side and back into the woods a bit. Not sure when or why. I think my great-grandma Betty realized that Doris was the most vulnerable and probably should get out of that institution as soon as possible. After the application process and home visits, Doris, at age sixteen, was finally able to go home to her family on July 7 of 1933. Her Grandma Betty was sixty-eight years old at that time. Doris had been institutionalized for nearly three years.

April 25, 1933. *Summary of State Agent's Special Report, Doris Norgren, Age 16*

Mrs. Betty Norgren was residing in Palmers Township in St. Louis County and had applied for her granddaughter, Doris Norgen to be placed with her. Mrs. Norgren's home is described as a "small house, covered with tar paper but finished nicely inside," similar to others in the area. The furnishings are described as "fair," and the home had some books and periodicals, as well as a piano and organ. Schooling promised was "thru 11th grade if she can get that far."

Further remarks: Mrs. Norgren, paternal grandmother of Doris Norgren, has always been interested in Doris and anxious to have her. She has remarked many times that she hoped to live until Doris is 18 so that she can have her with her then. I asked her if she would care to take Doris now and she seemed delighted with the prospect, and says that as long as she lives Doris can live with her.

John Norgren, Doris' brother has lived with his grandmother for a number of years and says he would like to have Doris come so he could go out and get a job. As it is, he must stay near home so as to be with his grandmother nights so she won't be alone. He says Doris would have a good home there and plenty to eat.

They own 5 acres of land and have a fine garden in summer and chickens the year round and plenty of fish. They live on the highway between Two Harbors and Duluth and just the highway is between them and Lake Superior.

The grandmother has some insurance left from her husband and gets help from a married son in Duluth and relatives live just next door to them. All seem to help each other and they have no worry about being able to care for Doris.

The home was clean and comfortable. They have two rooms down and two upstairs. Doris would sleep in the grandmother's room in a bed by herself. Doris can attend school every day...
(Appendix Q)

FLOSSY SENT SMALL gifts to her siblings that she had to leave behind at the orphanage. Dougal, Albert and Doris. There are many little notes throughout the two file boxes that I was privy to. The children of John Otto and Mary McNeill Norgren really did love one another, as best they could after all that they had been through.

Florence sent her siblings Christmas gifts. The Sandwicks, the woman who was the housekeeper for John Otto when he was still alive and who also helped get the children sent to the orphanage, also sent gifts. Another "RECEIVED OF" note showed a gift of $1.00 for Doris from older brother John from French River where John Otto's mother, (John Wendell's grandmother) Betty lived. John went to live with her after John Otto was killed.

IV

The below note is the only piece of State Public School documentation that I have regarding my Uncle Dougal. We used to visit Uncle Dougal and his wife, Aunty Doris, often, at their home in Two Harbors. To clarify, I had a blood-related Aunty Doris (red hair) and a by-marriage-related Aunty Doris (married to Uncle Dougal). It reads:

> Owatonna Minn
> Sept 19, 1931
> Dear Deward Norgren,
> I am feeling fine and hope you are the same. I saw a whale. He weighed 68 tons and was 56 feet long. They got 3,000 gallons of blood that was a giant whale. It took 16 hours to catch him. Say hello to them all down there, I'll close with love
> Your brother, Dougal Norgren

Dougal was eleven years old when he wrote this.

V

(Author's note: I think this might be the Mrs. Olson that was considering taking Doris in, but changed her mind because of the girl's physical issues.)

June 12, 1930. *Letter from State Agent to Galen Marrill, Superintendent, Minnesota State School*

Dear Mr. Merrill,

I have today visited and investigated the home of Carl E. Olson who applied for Albert Norgren. The home is average - clean and comfortable but no luxuries. Mr. Olson is a bridge builder and has charge of a crew for the railroad. He is a good workman and well liked by his superiors. Mr. Norgren was one of his workmen and had asked him several times to take Albert but refused to let him be adopted and so nothing came of it. Mr. Olson feels a certain obligation towards the boy now and not having any children it is natural that they want him. Mr. Olson at one time was in the habit of going on sprees and being missing from home for several days at a time, but he has quit this habit and has apparently quit drinking entirely. Mrs. Olson is a fine woman but is a Catholic and wants to know if she will have to bring the boy up a Protestant. I told her that this was our rule. She has no objection to this but feels that the boy will naturally adopt her religion, as Mr. Olson seldom goes to church, while she goes regularly. She asked if they could legally adopt him and if our rule would then apply. I told her that they would probably be refused permission to adopt because of their religious situation and that it would be much better for them to take a Catholic boy. Judge Scott is quite determined that they shall have Albert and they also prefer him, as they have had him in their home before. Mrs. Olson is not opposed to raising him Protestant as they were not married by a

priest and so have made no promises about children. I believe that it will be safe to approve the application as all the boy's relatives are Protestants and live all around them.
(Appendix R)

Between the time of the recommendation to place Albert at the Olsons and his actual physical move to their home his right clavicle was fractured. There is no report of how that happened. (Appendix S). There are quite a few reports in Hospital records of skin eruptions for all the children (1930-1933).

On August 2nd the Olsons' agreement to take Albert in was noted. After 14 days things fell apart.

VI

August 16, 1930. *Letter from Mrs. Carl E. Olson to Galen Marrill, Superintendent, Minnesota State School*

Mr. Galen A Merrill
Supt Minn State School
Owatonna Minn

Dear Sir,
　　According to our agreement for Albert Norgren, kindly advise me what to do.
　　Mr. Olson, my husband, had a terrible speeder accident yesterday - the 15th. His speeder jumped the track with himself and six of his men. He got both legs broken and both ankles smashed. He will be laid up a year or 18 months. I am obliged to go out and work for that time if not longer. The boy would have

to be shifted from one place to another. I myself think it more advisable to return him before we get further attached to him, as he is a little wonder, and if he is not placed into some home, in the meantime, we would take him back as soon as Mr. Olson is well and we are able to give him what is reasonable.

Kindly advise me what to do, as I want the proper thing done for the boy.

Thanking you, I am.
Mrs. Carl E. Olson

Albert had only twenty-seven days with this first family. The weight of finding these documents was immense for me. I never got to meet my Uncle Albert.

Poor Albert, getting sent back to the orphanage and state public school. His first-grade report card (1930-1931) shows a series of F (75-80) and U (below 75) grades. (Appendix T)

BY THIRD GRADE Albert was doing better. Not sure what "Withdrew Dec 5" means but he may have been farmed out. Have I explained what "Farmed Out" means? You had better sit down for this one. If you have ever read anything about the Orphan Trains, you already have a good idea of what it means. It is placing a boy with a family on a farm, to work as a farm hand for his room and board. These were very young boys often being treated like animals or slaves in the farms, beaten and worked to the bone. Punishment for not working hard enough or long enough was, too often, to withhold food. Too often, love and belonging were not part of it and, horribly, sexual assault was.

Albert was farmed out several times, moving from one bad family to another. He did stay for quite a while at one home or farm but he was found to be very small, underweight by quite a bit. Once they did move him to the last place, he gained weight and seemed happier but, the situations were dire at times for many farmers, and his last family was losing their farm.

Albert was either removed from, or ran away from, every place they sent him. The further story is below. If you are as softhearted as I am, you may want to jump ahead. I cried and had nightmares. I feel it all so personally, so deeply. My good imagination and my own story tend to help me with that.

October 2, 1939. *Letter from Albert Norgren to Mr. Hoel*

Alberta, Minnesota

> Dear Mr. Hoel, I am going to leave Siebrecht's and work for myself. I am not satisfied with the home any more than they're satisfied with my work.
>
> As you know, I have been to three homes and have not been able to hold onto none of them.
>
> Mrs. Siebrecht asked me to remain until you had found me a new place, but I do not wish to enter a new place. I do not think I'll be any more satisfactory there than in the other places.
>
> Do not worry about me for there are two or three things I have in mind and I think I'll succeed in one of them.
>
> I am writing this letter so you won't blame the Siebrecht's for what I'm to blame for. They don't know where I'm going, that's my worry now.
>
> Albert Norgren

THIS BOY, BEAUTIFUL, gentle and strong, Albert refused to be treated like an animal. He fought for his freedom again and again. I bet his kids have no idea of what he went through, because oftentimes, and especially for males, grit shows no weakness. He held it all in, never letting it out to hurt or damage the ones that are young and loved beyond any love that had been shown to this courageous, battered boy. This gentle loving child was sent to abusive farm after abusive farm. His battle with this system was ferocious. To attain his freedom from it was all that mattered to him. He would not be held prisoner any longer. He tried hard to work within this backwards system, wishing and hoping to fit in and stay, but he finally gave up and hid until he was of age to be free to join his injured but determined siblings again.

All of these amazing humans continued to love one another. Even though life didn't allow them the freedom to stay close, they loved deeply and dealt with it all ever so courageously.

Part 8
Closing Thoughts

I

Before I got the documents from the State Public Schools, I was completely unaware that my grandmother was put into an institution such a long time before my grandfather was killed. Until I had the files and started putting the pieces together, I thought that this all happened simultaneously or in very close succession. I had been under the impression that my mother was three or four years old when it all happened. Now I know that she was not even two years old for what we think was the second drowning attempt. That means that all the stories I thought she was remembering, and telling me, were second-hand, told to her by her siblings and probably her adoptive parents from their point of view, though I have heard some people say they remember things from when they were that young.

She was five years old when she entered the orphanage. That also came to me as quite a shock and I worried about all that time in between, hoping for the best, as I continued to study and piece together the State Public School Records.

It took me a very long time to get through it all, as it was so emotional for me and not in chronological order. It held so much more information than I ever thought I would have, having been given my mother's file box but finding so much information about her siblings, the child welfare system, and the participants within it. There were still many huge gaping holes in the story that kept me up at night wondering and creating scenarios to try to fill in the gaps.

The more I read and studied the documents, the more I longed to be there with them, to know and feel their experiences. I longed to understand how they survived, and if they could thrive after so much trauma. There were times when I found the truth so jarring that I had to step away for a time to rest my head and heart. Some breaks from this took years, as life was full and busy, and often a struggle just to get and keep enough money coming in to live.

Gaining so much information about the Owatonna State Public School and Home for Neglected and Abandoned Children was a very hard pill to swallow. Knowing that five of John and Mary's children, the youngest being my mom, were ripped from their siblings and dropped into another violent mess was another dose of trauma for me to work through. Once I started to realize the enormity of this state-run institution, and the number of years it was allowed to operate, it felt too heavy to visit every day, through reading the documents and writing. So unhealthy and unfriendly for thousands of children along with the trauma of working there if you were a gentle soul.

My story's a handful of battered, and now legally, physically and emotionally abandoned and orphaned children, would later become my mother and my aunts and my uncles. All of us, their children, still carry their traumas.

They were sent to that faraway institution after all they had already been through. It wasn't a home, it was a prison with torture and more trauma than one can even imagine.

How far from happy and healthy it was in the homes some of them did get to finish their growing up in. And those that had to move in and out of foster homes, never having real stability, which only more deeply secured the lasting trauma. The messages of who they were and what they deserved were being deeply embedded. How many lifetimes does it take to work all that out?

This was the story that I asked to know, longed to find and needed to look at and feel. I remain grateful for this path that chose me, though it is so draining to revisit and rewrite. I am the deeply feeling one of my siblings, the only one that is drawn to know, though I am learning more about cousins that have the same pull to this history of ours.

It amazes me that these children came out as well as they did, but I really knew only my mom and Flossy up close and personally. I did get to be around my Uncle Dougal as he and my mom were very close, in age and at heart. I know his children and their children, and was around his wife, my Auntie Doris, many times in my life. They were not trouble free, nor perfectly behaved parents, but they were deeply loving, and I find that amazing.

II

How, at twelve years old, do I know what I feel about the attempted murders of my mother and her siblings and the surrounding stories of my mother's existence prior to and after such a turning point? At age sixty-two I wonder where I would be now if there had been no such incidents? If life kept on like it had without my grandmother breaking from the strain of her life.

It is not clear at what age I started carrying this fault in my lineage. The weight of just being was quite heavy. From my start, a seven-year-old, not so mentally healthy sister, taking too much care of me, and our parents were drunks. We all suffered.

III

When we are consciously in our bodies, we know our connections to this life and each other. When we are hit or beaten as children, we learn to leave our bodies and live outside ourselves making it impossible to truly connect with others. Brutal words are just as powerful to keep us from being. Please reconsider your physical and emotional responses to all other living creatures, humans included. They create everything.

When creating the timeline for my visit with the two Knife River folks working in their yard, I panicked. I felt such anxiety about even discussing it with them I could hardly breathe, and had to flee. I could have stayed and learned more. I was not a grown-up on that day. It was big, feeling ready to look at the historical marker, to read it, to walk down those stairs to find the scene of the crime, but I was still a wreck. Why? Was it shame? I know part of it was. I've carried this family's bag of shame for as long as I can remember. Was it fear of learning the truth, good or bad? Of not being able to hang on to all this drama, of not having it be so important, so dramatic? What and who would I be without it? And then there is that ever-present fear of intruding, not being welcome or necessary.

How do I heal? Relive it, dive in and know it, believe it, understand the situation from the inside out from the perspective of all that it involves. Say "no" on the way in, and "yes" on the way out. And that over and over and over again.

This path is not for everyone, not by any means. And it doesn't not show anything about a person other than the avenues of one's curiosity about their own wounds and personality traits.

MY LIFE HAS been pretty amazing. Telling this story has been a big part of it. I filled in some of the blanks and created others. My deep desire to learn about those that share my DNA has led me to learn about myself. Of course it did. That is really why I did it.

I know that there are humans who cannot feel. I must feel, and I would imagine that the discomfort for those that don't feel is as extreme for them if and when they do.

Somehow, I gave myself permission to love all these people that shared their promise with me. They promised only to be.

IV

I was brought home from the hospital to a one-story light teal house on Avondale Street. The white front door opened in toward the living room, with a fairly large kitchen to the left. I remember the large picture window in the middle of the back wall of the living room, and the huge weeping willow that nearly filled the bottom half of the fairly long back yard. There was no alleyway behind it and no homes were built on the grassy land behind, so it felt quite open and wonderful when we played out there. I remember playing in the backyard, though we would not live in that house past my third birthday. I have a photograph of my younger sister in a buggy on the front walk. I and a few of the neighbor kids, Suzy and Perry Weatherby, and another I can't identify are all standing around her, waiting to have the shot taken.

At the beginning of writing this book I told you that I longed to find the truths, the traumas, the loves, and the losses of John Otto Norgren, my biological grandfather. As I started to close this out and feel for the resolutions and the finality of seeking, reading, sorting fact from fiction, data from mislabeled, or misdated documents and so many ways to spin all of this, I stopped dead in my tracks realizing that I had not found out enough about John Otto to really understand him.

I didn't uncover any of his truths and traumas. I know he was addicted to alcohol, that he was violent, worked hard but didn't support his family like he should have, and that is really all I still know. I was not able to find a clear history of my grandfather, John Otto Norgren's life before he was a womanizer and a drunk nor did I find any stories of his goodness that must have been there in some capacity.

There is a story regarding his being born in Sweden that I have not brought up because it has not been proven. I remember hearing about it when I was child. John Otto Norgren immigrated to the United States when he was three years old but the story was that my grandmother, Betty Norgren Sandberg, was impregnated by King Oscar II of Sweden and Norway, but was himself French. The story was that while working as a maid in his castle, she was had by him and then was given enough money to pay for her passage and sent away to America. We heard that story forever. I've pretty well decided that it isn't true, but there are others that still hold it to be. There are stark differences in his look, his hair color, skin and eyes, from the rest of his siblings.

I really don't know any more about him than I did when I started the research, seeking all the information I could find. For now, I'll have to be okay with that, and perhaps forever. It doesn't seem as important as it did when I started.

This collecting and sharing of what I did find was a long and meaningful journey of self-love and acceptance. It was fueled by a deep desire to allow the rest of my family the opportunity to see and feel the truth about how amazing our grandparents, our parents, sisters and brothers, uncles and aunts were. I think we all are pretty amazing. Their traumas and courage, their life experiences have shaped us. I get to take the deep sense of family kindness and love, the courage and true grit to carry on and to lovingly leave behind what doesn't serve me in this amazing life that I have been given. I wish you the same, or whatever you seek, that will serve you best. I will end by wishing for you what my mother wished for me so often: Have a beauty day.

Acknowledgements

Many people have contributed monetary gifts to make this publication possible. I wish to acknowledge them below: Ray Allard and Gerri Williams, Gary Anderson and Gary Boelhower, Jenny Bauer and Allen Constant, Steve Bauer and Suzanne Marcus, Dianna Bell, Ron Benson and Margaret Meagher, Bev Berntson, Terry and Dennis Dunham, Cindy French, Mara Hart, Al Kammerer and Susan Maher, Linda Kirchmaier, Gary Keveles, Gordon Levine, Marilyn Mayry, Judy Nelson, Jim Perlman, Candice Richards, Adeline Wright and Allen Killian-Moore.

Special thanks to Adeline Wright, Allen Killian-Moore, Meredith Cornett, and Mara Hart for their collective efforts to bring this story into production.

Interview with the Author

In the fall of 2022, Cathy Wright sat down with her daughter, Adeline Wright, for an interview. They talked about life, love, family and writing *Have a Beauty Day*.

AW: Who was your favorite musician?
CW: Elton John.

AW: What is your fondest memory?
CW: Smoking weed and driving up Seven Bridges Road with Joanie Hanson and Kim Talbot.

AW: What are your fears?
CW: Being stuck where I cannot really live. It's hard to recognize that I still have so many things that I want to or could do. I feel like I failed myself. I had no self-confidence.

AW: How many times were you in love?
CW: Zero. I chose men who I thought could give me a good life. It was more of a doing than a being. I didn't know how to love.

AW: What were some happy times in your life?
CW: Probably at the age of 14 or 15 walking in Lester Park, hanging out with friends, swimming in the Deeps.
    When I was 27 or 28, living in Duluth, recently graduated from Votech with a degree in Industrial Electrical Maintenance. I loved breaking barriers.

AW: What is something you are proud of?
CW: I'm proud of myself for digging in and healing as much as I could.

AW: How long did it take you to write this book?
CW: Approximately 15 years.

AW: If you could change one thing about your life, what would it be?
CW: Dementia—for myself and my mom.

AW: What is one thing you know to be true?
CW: Change isn't easy, but it's so fucking worth it!

AW: What was your first car?
CW: My grandfather's Buick Invicta: red body, cream top with big fenders.

AW: Where do you draw inspiration from?
CW: It feels important to document my experience of growing up and surviving an alcoholic family: trying to heal myself and my daughter.

AW: Who have your writing mentors been?
CW: Mara Hart and Adeline Wright.

AW: Do you view writing as a spiritual practice?
CW: Hell, yes! Not in a religious way but cultivating the energy that comes through discovering my ancestors' experiences.

I think I learned more than I'll ever be able to express by going to Al-Anon. I told my story and it healed me to a certain degree. My mother, Betty Wright, was an early leader within Al-Anon in Duluth, Minnesota.

Appendices: Selection of Original Historical Documents

A. Car Kills Two Harbors Railroad Worker on Road (April 23, 1930)
B. Letter from Galen A. Marrill to Judge W. E. Scott (May 9, 1930)
C. Response from Judge W. E. Scott to Galen A. Marrill (May 15, 1930)
D. Letter from Frank O'Malley to Galen A. Marrill (May 15, 1930)
E. The Child History (Betty Lois Norgren), Age 6
F. Agreement between the State Board of Control and William M. Hill (August 2, 1930)
G. Letter to Dr. William F. Smith of the Wilmar State Hospital from Phyllis M. Zamboni, Child Placing Agent at the Minnesota State Public School (November 10, 1932)
H. Response from Wilmar State Asylum to Phyllis M. Zamboni (November 12, 1932)
I. State Agent's Report, Betty Norgren, Age 6 (February 26, 1931)
J. State Agent's Report, Betty Norgren, Age 7 (October 21, 1932)
K. State Agent's Report, Betty Norgren, Age 11 (December 14, 1936)
L. State Agent's Report, Betty Norgren, Age 12 (July 22, 1937)
M. State Agent's Report, Betty Norgren, Age 13 (June 24, 1938)

N. State Agent's Report, Betty Norgren, Age 14 (October 12, 1939)
O. Letter from Judge W. E. Scott, Judge of Probate, Lake County to the State Public School in Owatonna, Minnesota (May 8, 1930)
P. Letter from Vernon Norgren to Doris Norgren (November 12, 1944)
Q. State Agent's Special Report, Doris Norgren, Age 16 (April 25, 1933)
R. Letter from Dougal Norgren to Deward Norgren (September 19, 1931)
S. Hospital Records, Albert Norgren (1930-1933)
T. Report Card, Albert Norgren, First Grade (1930-1931)

Appendix A
Car Kills Two Harbors Railroad Worker on Road
April 25, 1930

Car Kills Two Harbors Railroad Worker on Road
1930

TWO HARBORS, April 23.—(Special.)—J. O. Nordgren, crane operator for the D., M. & N. railroad company in the yards at Two Harbors was instantly killed at 8:30 p. m. today on state highway No. 1, one-half mile west of Two Harbors, when he stepped into the path of a passing automobile, driven by Ingwald Sandea, machinist helper in the local shops, who was on his way home on the Stanley rd. According to his report he saw the man walking off the highway on the side of the road and just as he got to him the man stepped into the path of the car. Sandea swung out but the fender of his car struck the man throwing him into the air and through the glass of the car door. Nordgren is survived by six children; his wife is in the state hospital at Fergus Falls. Sandea, after being questioned by police, was not held, but will appear at the coroner's inquest tomorrow morning.

My biological grandfather was killed. They spelled his name wrong. J. O. Nordgren is John Otto Norgren.

Appendix B
Letter from Galen A. Marrill to Judge W. E. Scott
May 9, 1930

May 9, 1930.

Hon. W. E. Scott,
Judge of Probate,
Two Harbors, Minn.

Dear Sir:

In answer to your letter of the 8th inst. relative to the Norgren children let me say that the five younger ones, namely Doris, Florence, Dougal, Betty and Albert, can be committed to this school and may be sent at any time on your order if you find them eligible to admission. I am enclosing some Child History blanks which you may use in recording information about their family history. Commitment may be made to the State Public School. The State Board of Control automatically becomes the personal guardian of children committed to this institution. If some of them are to be placed in homes I think it would be well for them to come here first and be examined and prepared for placement. The families wanting them will then be visited by one of our representatives with a view to make permanent arrangements for them.

Yours truly,

Galen A. Merrill,
Superintendent.

GAM:J

Appendix C
Response from Judge W. E Scott to Galen A. Marrill
May 15, 1930

W. E. SCOTT
JUDGE OF PROBATE

OFFICE OF
JUDGE OF PROBATE
LAKE COUNTY
TWO HARBORS, MINN.

May 15, 1930

Galen A. Merrill, Esq.
Superintendent
Minn. State Public School
Owatonna, Minn.

Dear Mr. Merrill: Attention: Mr. Merrill's Secretary

    Thank you for your letter of May 9 relative to the Norgren children. It is very probable that the children will be committed to the State Public School at Owatonna, and in that event, they will arrive in Owatonna the first of next week.

    There are four families here that have signified that they would like to each adopt one of the children. Accordingly, will you send me a few of your application blanks for children from your school?

    Mr. and Mrs. Frank O'Malley were in here this morning and they would like to adopt Florence. They wrote to you in connection with this and you have no doubt received the letter by this time. I believe the O'Malleys would provide a very good home for the children.

    Another family that I feel certain would provide well for a child is that of Mr. and Mrs. William Hill. I would most heartily recommend that Betty be placed with them if they so desire.

    We trust that you will give your sympathetic consideration to the applications which come in for these children from Two Harbors.

Yours very truly,

W. E. Scott
Judge of Probate.

Appendix D
Letter from Frank O'Malley to Galen A. Marrill
May 15, 1930

524-Third Avenue
Two Harbors, Minn.
May 15, 1930

Mr. Galen A. Merrill, Supt.
Minn. State Public School
Owatonna, Minn.

Dear Mr. Merrill: Attention: Mr. Merrill's Secretary

   I understand that five children of the Norgren family will probably go down to your school for placement the first part of next week. Mrs. O'Malley and I are very anxious to adopt one of the little children, namely, Florence. Will you be kind enough to send us an application blank so we may make a formal request?

   Mr. W. E. Scott, Judge of Probate, tried to get you on the long distance phone in regard to this matter this morning, but you were out of town. He will phone you again on Saturday to explain the circumstances.

   The children are going to Owatonna with Miss Nellie Swanson, welfare worker for the Duluth, Missabe & Northern Ry. Co. If Mrs. O'Malley goes down with her, and conditions are satisfactory, may she bring Florence back with her at once?

   Perhaps you can get a written reply back to us by Monday.

Yours very truly,
Frank O'Malley

Appendix E (page 1 of 4)
The Child History (Betty Lois Norgren), Age 6
1930

B. of C. Form 69B—Child and Family History Record.

The Child History

8698

Full Name __Betty Lois Norgren__ Address __Two Harbors, Minnesota__
Color __white__ Legitimate __yes__ Date of Birth __Jan. 15, 1925__
Place of Birth __Knife River, Minn.__ Religion __Lutheran__ Baptized Date __1929__ Place __Two Harbors__ Confirmed ___
Age entered school __6 yrs.__ Age left school __In school__ Grade at leaving __Kindergarden__
Address of last school attended __Two Harbors__ Reason for leaving ___

Age child entered employment __---__ Reason for entering __---__

Names and addresses of employers	Length of time employed by each and date of employment	Wage

Does child attend church or Sunday School __yes__ Name and address of pastor __Rev. O.M. Bloom, Two Harbors, Minn.__
Result of physical examination of child (What physician has examined) __Good condition, examined by school nurse, Miss Georgia Eldridge.__
Diseases, temporary or chronic, abnormalities or deformities, etc., __none__

Result of mental examination, name of examiner. (Insanity, feeblemindedness, epilepsy, intelligence quotient, etc.)
__Otis Test, 97__

Has this child been inmate of any institution __no__ Has this child ever been in jail? __no__
Name of institution-jail __---__
Address ___
Date of entry ___ Date left ___ How and by whom sent ___

Is child known to any social or charitable agency?
Name of __Nallie M. Swanson__ Address __110 Wolven Bldg. Duluth, Minn.__ Date ___
Has child any record of crime, delinquency (incorrigibility, immorality, truancy). State places and dates, brief summary of facts (court records, if any) __Duluth, Missabe & Northern Ry. Co.__
__None__

Appendix E (page 2 of 4)

Moral History—crime, delinquency, immorality, etc. (If arrested or in Court, give dates and places) (dates and places of sentence to penal institutions, names of institutions) (specify for father and mother)
None

Present environment of home and neighborhood Fair

Family known to any social or charitable agency? Date and places At present to Miss Nellie Swanson, welfare worker, Duluth, Missabe & Northern Ry. Co.

Amount of education of father and mother—standards of home Not known--see reports on Parents

Church attendance Lutheran

Children: *(Other than child whose history appears elsewhere on this blank.)*
Have any of the children temporary or chronic diseases, abnormalities or deformities, etc.? (Specify children by name and give character of difficulty.)
No

Are any of the children insane, feebleminded, epileptic or of low mental grade? (Specify children by name.)
No information

Do any of the children have a record of crime, delinquency, immorality, truancy? (Give dates, places, and specify facts.) If any are or have been in institutions, give dates and places.
No

State of Minnesota
County of Lake
IN JUVENILE COURT
In the Matter of Betty Norgren
dependent child
CHILD AND FAMILY HISTORY RECORD
Filed this _____ day of _____ A. D. 19___
_____ Judge of Probate
_____ County, Minn.

Appendix E (page 3 of 4)

Form 146 2-26—2M

OWATONNA STATE PUBLIC SCHOOL

Case No. 3698

SBC No. ....

STATISTICAL

Child's Name: Betty Lois Norgren
Date committed: May 19, 1930
Date Admitted: May 20, 1930
Residence: Two Harbors, Minn.
County: Lake
Age or Date of Birth: Jan. 15, 1925
By Order Court: Juvenile - Lake County
Birthplace: Knife River, Minn.
Judge: W.S. Scott
Sex: Female Color: White
By Transfer from:
Petitioners: Mrs. John Sandwick
Address:

Relationship of Petitioners: None
Cause of Dependency: Death of father

Contributory Causes: Insanity of mother

HISTORICAL

Name of School: Minnehaha, Grade: Kind., Years Attended: , Last Attended: 5-19-30
Cause of Leaving: Committed to S.P.S.
Teacher: Miss Lowe
Church: Lutheran - Baptised at Two Harbors in 1929
Sunday School:
Previous Environment:

Associates, Names and Character:

Habits:

PHYSICAL CHARACTERISTICS

Prenatal History:

Birth History:

Physical Condition when admitted: Good - Has had whooping cough, mumps, measles and scarlet fever - (reported by Doris and Florence).

Injuries or Operations:

Appendix E (page 4 of 4)

8698			DETENTION		Entered 5-20-30 H	
Name Betty Lois Norgren			Age 1-15-25 Sex Female		Left	
Date	Height	Weight	Eyes R. 20/	L. 20/	Ears R. 20/	L. 20/
5-21-30	41½	36	+/−1 Scalp ✓		Skin ✓	
			+/− Glands ✓		Hernia ✓	
			+/− Nose ✓		Throat ✓	
			+/− Teeth		Tonsils 3	
			+/− Heart ✓		Lungs ✓	
			+/− Speech ✓		Nutrition ✓	
Toxin-Antitox.	1st 5-26-30		2nd 6-2-30		3rd 6-9-30	
Vaccination	1st recent vaccination		2nd		3rd	

Remarks 5/21/30 N+T Culture to S.B.H neg. 4/1/30 Mantoux T.B.N to 0.01 mgm neg. 4/1/30 T.B.N to 0.1 mgm neg.

Appendix F
Agreement between the State Board of Control and William H. Hill
August 2, 1930

#8698

Minnesota State Public School

This Agreement, By and Between the State Board of Control, party of the first part, and .... William M. Hill .... of the town of .... Two Harbors .... Section .... County of .... Lake .... State of Minnesota, Post Office address 227 So. Ave., Two Harbors party of the second part.

WITNESSETH, That said Board, in consideration of the agreement herein made by said second party, hereby places .... Betty Lois Norgren .... one of the wards of this Board, in the family of said second party to remain until the .... 15th .... day of .... January .... 1943, when said child will be 18 years of age, reserving the right to cancel this agreement, and require the child to be returned to this school, whenever, in the opinion of said Board, the conditions of this agreement are not faithfully executed or when otherwise the interest of said child requires it.

The said second party hereby reserves the right to cancel this agreement at any time within ninety days from the date of the same by returning the said child at his own expense to this school.

The said second party receives said child into his family and agrees to keep h..er.. until the said .... 15th .... day of .... January .... 1943, maintaining, educating and treating h..er.. properly and kindly as a member of his family; to provide h..er.. with suitable and sufficient clothing for week days and for attending public religious worship and with suitable food and other necessaries in health and sickness; to have h..er.. taught an occupation to enable h..er.. to become self supporting and the branches usually taught in the common schools, causing h..er.. to attend the public school where he resides, fully complying with the compulsory school laws of Minnesota. At the termination of this agreement he will furnish said child with two good suits of clothes and will pay for the benefit of said child, on the order of the Superintendent of said school, the sum of .... One Hundred Dollars .... or wages as per the following terms: .... ($100.00) ....

.... If said child shall not remain in his family the full term of this agreement he will pay pro rata for the time .. she does .. remain, such pro rata to be paid promptly when the agreement is terminated.

In case this agreement shall be cancelled by either party, as aforesaid, the second party agrees to return said child to this school at his own expense.

Whenever requested by the Superintendent or an Agent of said school, the said second party agrees to report to him in writing, such facts in regard to said child as he shall request, and that he will furnish said child with materials and opportunity to correspond with said Superintendent or Agent. In case said second party changes his place of residence or his post office address during the time said child remains in his family he agrees immediately to notify said Superintendent.

IN WITNESS THEREOF, The said State Board of Control by the Superintendent of this Institution, and said second party, hereby set their names and seals this .... 2nd .... day of .... August 1930 .... *Galen A. Merrill* .... (L. S.)
Superintendent of State Public School.
.... *William M. Hill* .... (L. S.)

Appendix G
Letter to Dr. William F. Smith of the Wilmar State Hospital from Phyllis M. Zamboni, Child Placing Agent at the Minnesota State Public School
November 10, 1932

MINNESOTA
STATE PUBLIC SCHOOL

November 10, 1932.

Betty Norgren-8698.

Dr. B. F. Smith,
Wilmar State Hospital,
Wilmar, Minnesota.

My dear Dr. Smith:

Upon the request of the foster parents of Betty Norgren, ward of this institution, I am writing you for a report of the condition of Betty's mother, Mary Norgren, aged 44 who was committed to The Wilmar State Hospital about 1928.

We should appreciate a summary of the patient's social and medical history—with a statement of the mental diagnosis upon admission, subsequent changes in diagnosis, her response to treatment, and the present prognosis.

Thank you for your helpfulness.

Sincerely yours,

Phyllis M. Zamboni,
Child Placing Agent.

Appendix H
Response from Willmar State Asylum to Phyllis M. Zamboni
November 12, 1932

WILLMAR STATE ASYLUM
DR. B. F. SMITH, Superintendent
WILLMAR, MINNESOTA

Nov. 12, 1932

Subject: Mary Norgren

#8694

RECEIVED
NOV 14 1932
STATE PUBLIC SCHOOL
OWATONNA, MINNESOTA

Miss Phyllis M. Zamboni,
Minnesota State Public School,
Owatonna, Minnesota.

Dear Madam:

    Your letter of November 10th concerning Mrs. Mary Norgren has been received. She was committed to the Fergus Falls State Hospital in September, 1926. The date of her birth is 1887. She attended the 5th grade in school and her religion is protestant. Her mental diagnosis is Dementia Praecox, Hebephrenic type. Her commitment history gives the following information and it is about 3 years and 7 months previous to admission to Fergus Falls.

    "First symptoms about one year ago. She was nervous and neglected her housework and children. Religious. Imagines some injury to her head. Threatened her children and husband. She was very religious. She was in the county jail for three days."

Fergus Falls State Hospital gives the following information on her while she was there.

    "On admission she was delusional, her delusions being of a sexual nature. She had ideas that she had relations with her nine year old girl, etc. She had ideas that her husband had relations with her nine year old daughter and that he was unfaithful and kept company with other women. She is listless, indifferent, shows no capacity for employment and scolds at times. Her sister Lillian Bucher is a patient at this hospital."

    Her appetite is good and she sleeps well. She takes considerable interest in her surroundings and attends picture shows and chapel services at the institution. Her conversation is rambling and incoherent on some subjects. She continues to be delusional and at times will attack the nurses. Her present weight is 192 pounds.

        Very truly yours,

        Superintendent.

BFS/MR

Appendix I
State Agent's Report, Betty Norgren, Age 6
February 26, 1931

Rec. No. 8698   Born 1-15-25   Adm. 5-20-30   Placed 8-2-30

State Agent's Report

Two Harbors, Minnesota, Feb. 26, 1931

To the Superintendent of the State Public School,

Owatonna, Minnesota.

Dear Sir:

The following is a statement of the facts, as far as I have ascertained them, regarding Betty Norgren aged 6 years, one of the wards of the State Public School, living with Wm M Hill in Lake County, whom I have this day visited. The child was personally seen and talked with by me.

1. Child's physical condition excellent
2. Has attended school during the past year all months.
3. Progress in school is good
4. Studies 1st Grade
5. Has attended Church and Sunday School yes
6. The child's work is play
7. Its moral condition is good usually — has been quite a problem though & they had some trouble with her at school, but is improving.
8. Is it contented? yes
9. Is it liked by guardian? yes
10. The guardian's treatment of child is very good
11. The general impression of the home is good city home
12. Recommendations and remarks Mr. Hill has wood working machinery & makes useful furniture for Betty — She has so many nice things to play with — writing desk, kitchen cabinet, kitchen utensils & dolls — buggy and many more useful things. They will not adopt Betty as so many of her relatives are insane.

M. Goodrich
State Agent

Appendix J (page 1 of 2)
State Agent's Report, Betty Norgren, Age 7
October 21, 1932

Rec. No. 8698   Born 1-15-25   Adm. 5-20-30   Placed 8-2-30

State Agent's Report

Two Harbors, Minnesota, October 21, 1932

To the Superintendent of the State Public School,
Owatonna, Minnesota.

Dear Sir:

The following is a statement of the facts, as far as I have ascertained them, regarding Betty Norgren Wise aged 7 years, one of the wards of the State Public School, living with Mrs. H. xx Wise in ___ in ___, County, whom I have this day visited. The child was ___. Personally seen and talked with by me.

1. Child's physical condition Child eats and sleeps well – has plenty of outdoor play. Is 2 lbs underweight. Dr. Bernd of Two Harbors gives medical supervision.
2. Has attended school during the past year 9 months.
3. Progress in school is Rapid – grade ahead of her age – given help at home.
4. Studies 3rd grade.
5. Has attended Church and Sunday School Regularly
6. The child's work is
7. Its moral condition is Satisfactory. Parents are inclined to be overly-anxious about her school progress.
8. Is it contented? Yes.
9. Is it liked by guardian? Immensely. So devoted they are jealous of her interest in others.
10. The guardian's treatment of child is Try to give her the right training and establish wholesome regular habits of living.
11. The general impression of the home is Modern, well furnished home. Betty has her own room. Mrs. H. a good housekeeper.
12. Recommendations and remarks Mrs. H. welcomed the V. as many problems have been weighing on her mind. She is eager to safeguard Betty from her sister Florence who lives three blocks away. V. pointed out that it was only natural that the sisters should be interested in one another, and the surest way to strengthen the bond between

State Agent.

the children, which is the Hill's fear, is to make a place restrictions on the sisters seeing one another. Mrs. H. also wondered whether there was any advantage to their postponing adoption until Betty is 12 yrs. old, to be sure her development will be normal. Betty has been given 2 mental tests and was slightly above average on both tests. V. advised that her school work too showed her to have more than average mentality and the possibility of her carrying any taint from the mother, which would develop before she was an adult was very improbable. Mrs. H. requested a report on the mother's condition. Betty has shown no signs of instability. Enuresis cleared up after a yr. in her foster home. Mrs. H. asked V. advice regarding having Betty repeat 3rd grade so she would not advance too rapidly. Advised Mrs. H. to let school promotions go along naturally and let her pass if she showed a capacity for higher grade work. Mrs. H. said Betty was a gay, happy child — she has a good disposition — is eager to please and responds well to praise. She tries to be helpful about the house. Child is very neat and clean about her personal appearance.

P. M. Zamboni

Appendix K
State Agent's Report, Betty Norgren, Age 11
December 14, 1936

Rec. No. 3698 Born 1-15-25 Adm. 5-20-30 Placed 8-2-30

State Agent's Report

To the Superintendent of the State Public School Date of Visit Dec. 14, 1936 193__
Owatonna, Minnesota Date of Report Dec. 18, 1936 193__

Dear Sir:

The following is a statement of the facts, as far as I have ascertained them, regarding
__Betty Norgren__ aged (11) years, one of the wards of the State Public School.
Living with __Mr. K. Hill__
at __Two Harbors__ County __Lake__
whom I have this day visited. The child was __yes__ personally seen and talked with by me.

1. The child's physical condition is __very good, has been growing but still has headaches.__
2. Grade in school __6th__ Attendance __regular__ Progress __good__
3. Church and Sunday School attendance __regular__ Attitude toward Church __interested__
4. The child's work is __helpsome with the housework__
5. The child's moral attitude is __good girl__
6. Is the child contented? __yes__ Is the child liked by guardian? __yes__
7. The guardian's treatment of the child is __very good__
8. The general impression of the home is: Good __yes__ Less Desirable _____ Poor _____
   (Please Check)
   Child doing Well __yes__ Fairly Well _____ Poorly _____
   (Please Check)
9. Recommendations and remarks:

Betty is becoming a fine looking girl and very well mannered. She is lady like and polite, can sit down and visit and show an interest in other things besides her own doings. She still has headaches, Mrs. Hill calls them migrane headaches, and says the doctor says they are quite common among children born of parents who become insane.

Betty is not an especially good student but with help at home, they see that she keeps up with her grades. She prefers the out door sports to studying while at home. Mrs. Hill is very exact and wants to do just the right thing and so sees to it that the girl does some work at home around the house. She is also very much interested in church work, the whole family is, and just now all are working for Christmas. Mr. Hill, Chief of Police Dep't, spends his fall and early winter making toys for families for Christmas. They showed me his work shop in the basement and all the toys he had ready for the big church party. He does unusually fine work and his toys and small pieces of furniture last for many years as they are made so substantial. Among the pieces he had ready were, small cedar chests, doll beds and cradles, kitchen cupboards and cabinets, tables, chairs, wagons, carts, and toys of all kinds. He makes them for the church and on Christmas eve they are distributed to the poor families. The church gave him $10 this year for the material used.

This is an interesting home to visit although Mrs. Hill rather resents anyone coming in and snooping around or bossing as she says some people call it. She is always very friendly but she shows that she feels they can care for the girl without advice. She does not have the girl visit the others of her own family who live around there and they think she should be more intimate with them but she feels that she just doesn't have the time to keep up with all the girl's relatives and so they keep away from them. Betty sees her sister at school some times.

M. Goodrich
State Agent

Appendix L
State Agent's Report, Betty Norgren, Age 12
July 22, 1936

Rec. No. 9698 Born 1-15-25 Adm. 5-20-30 Placed 8-2-30

State Agent's Report

To the Superintendent of the State Public School   Date of Visit July 22, 193_7_
Owatonna, Minnesota

Dear Sir: Date of Report July 25, 193_7_

The following is a statement of the facts, as far as I have ascertained them, regarding

................Betty Norgren................ aged 12 years, one of the wards of the State Public School.

Living with ....William M. Hill..............

at ....Two Harbors............ County ...Lake...

whom I have this day visited. The child was yes personally seen and talked with by me.

1. The child's physical condition is very good, has very few headaches now
2. Grade in school 7th Attendance regular Progress good
3. Church and Sunday School attendance regular Attitude toward Church interested
4. The child's work is helps at home and this summer is working for a neighbor a few hours a day
5. The child's moral attitude is good girl
6. Is the child contented? yes Is the child liked by guardian? yes
7. The guardian's treatment of the child is very good
8. The general impression of the home is good city home - child doing well
9. Recommendations and remarks Betty is a nice girl and getting along all right. She is very enthusiastic about earning money this summer and is helping out at a neighbors caring for a little child and doing light housework. She works about 4 or 5 hours a day. She gets $1.50 a week and is saving it. She won't spend it unless for something she needs, bought a rain cape lately.

They reported that Florence, who was with Mr. and Mrs. O'Malley, in Two Harbors, left their home the night she graduated from High School in June and went to Duluth to do housework. Her sisters and brothers were there to see her graduate and took her back to Duluth with them. Doris, who was with the grandmother at Knife River, is also doing housework in Duluth.

The children are all trying to get together and don't seem to like it because the Hills do not let Betty visit with them as often as they would like. They want to keep her with them.

M. Goodrich
State Agent

Appendix M
State Agent's Report, Betty Norgren, Age 13
June 24, 1938

Rec. No. 8698 Born 1-15-25 Adm. 5-20-30 Placed 8-2-30

State Agent's Report

To the Superintendent of the State Public School   Date of Visit June 24, 1938

Owatonna, Minnesota   Date of Report June 26, 1938

Dear Sir:

The following is a statement of the facts, as far as I have ascertained them, regarding Betty Norgren aged 13 years, one of the wards of the State Public School. Living with Mr. Hill at Two Harbors, Minn. (City) County Lake whom I have this day visited. The child was (yes) personally seen and talked with by me.

1. The child's physical condition is _very good_
2. Grade in school _9th_ Attendance _regular_ Progress _good_
3. Church and Sunday School attendance _none_ Attitude toward Church _Disinterested_
4. The child's work is _helps at home_
5. The child's moral attitude is _seems good - no complaints_

6. Is the child contented? _yes_ Is the child liked by guardian? _yes_
7. The guardian's treatment of the child is _very good_

8. The general impression of the home is Good _X_ Less Desirable _____ Poor _____
   (Please Check)

   Child doing Well _X_ Fairly Well _____ Poorly _____
   (Please Check)

9. Recommendations and remarks:

   Betty is growing up into a fine looking girl. She stays at home most of the time & helps with the housework & with the garden. The whole family seems to prefer home to visiting around.

   Mr. Hill, Policeman, works nights but spends some time each day in his basement shop making furniture & children's toys. Mrs. Hill loves flowers & a garden & spends her time there.

   They do not visit the other Norgren children & relatives. Betty sees Florence occasionally. She has returned to the O'Malley home in Two Harbors & is keeping house for Mr. O'Malley as his wife died last year.

   Betty has a good home & is satisfied & contented there.

   M. Goodrich
   State Agent

Appendix N
State Agent's Report, Betty Norgren, Age 14
October 12, 1939

REPORT OF HOME VISIT

Rec. No. 8698 ... Born 1-15-25 ... Admitted 5-20-30 ... Placed 8-2-30
Concerning: Date of Visit Oct. 12, 1939
Betty Norgren ... Date of Report Oct. 31, 1939
.... aged 14 years, living with
William Hill .... at Two Harbors, Minn.

Was the child personally seen and talked with? no ...... County Lake
1. Type of placement: Adopt. ...... Free X ...... Wage ...... Rel. ...... Board. ...... Other
2. Location of home: City X ...... Town ...... Farm ...... Suburban or Lake ...... Other
3. Physical condition very good now
4. Grade in school 9th ...... Attendance regular ...... Progress good
5. Church and S. S. attendance regular ...... Name of church Lutheran
6. Child's work: Field ...... Chores ...... Housework X ...... Too young ...... Other
7. Case worker's evaluation:
    Is child contented? yes .... Is child liked by guardian? yes
    Estimate of child: Good X ...... Fair ...... Poor
    Estimate of home: Good X ...... Fair ...... Poor
    Estimate of child's
    adjustment to home: Good X ...... Fair ...... Poor

    There was no school the afternoon I called at the house and Betty had been allowed to go with the other school girls for the afternoon and so I did not see her.

    Mrs. Hill reports that Betty is doing well in school, and is a good girl and there are no complaints. She has lately been visiting with her sisters and brothers in the community and so has finally made some contact with them which was not approved of while she was younger.

    The sister who lived in another home in Two Harbors, is now married and Betty visits her occasionally. The others of the family visit the married sister and then Betty is invited thereto so she has a chance to see them all.

    They say that Albert Norgren is with his brother Deerwood who is married and living in Duluth.

M. Goodrich

Appendix O
Letter from Judge W. E. Scott, Judge of Probate, Lake County to the State Public School in Owatonna, Minnesota
May 8, 1930

May 8, 1930

State Public School
Owatonna, Minn.

Gentlemen:

There is a case in Two Harbors in regard to which we want to ask your advice.

There is a family here of eight children as follows:

    Deward Norgren --- 18 years
    Vernon Norgren   16 "
    John Norgren   15 "
    Doris Norgren   13 "
    Florence Norgren   11 "
    Dougal Norgren   9 "
    Betty Norgren   5 "
    Albert Norgren   6 "

The oldest boy, Deward, is taking care of himself and works at the Steel Plant at Duluth. The other seven children are attending the public schools here.

The mother of the children is at the State Hospital at Willmar and is unable to take care of them. The father of the children, namely John Otto Norgren, was killed in an automobile accident April 23, 1930.

Will you kindly advise us what should be done in a case like this? May the children be sent to the State school at Owatonna? If so, are they committed directly to your school and, if not committed, how should they be committed?

It appears that some of the children could be placed with families here in Two Harbors. In that event would the children still remain wards of the state?

As this is an urgent case, we would deeply appreciate a quick reply as well as any further information you may give us which will help us solve this problem to the best interest of the children.

Yours very truly,

W. E. Scott
Judge of Probate

Appendix P (page 1 of 4)
Letter from Vernon Norgren to Doris Norgren
November 12, 1944

Nov. 12, 1944
Somewhere in Europe

Dear Doris:

Recieved your welcome letter and was glad to hear that things are not to bad. Marie had said that Dougal would be home but he never writes. I did finally heard from Gilbert. It tough here and we have to be rugged but I am still well and all in one piece. We've seen about three months of action – more than I bargained for. We still hope to get it over with before to long.

We've watched the bombers come and go and the buzz bombers come but don't know where they are going. It's quiet a contraption.

It's damp and cold now and the outlook not to good for a comfortable winter. I dread these long dark nights very much. Not the best way to injoy life after thirty but I think we're putting the finnish on Hitler's outfit so it's not in vain.

There is not to much to write about and stay in our limits. The people here ar very industious and not to bad off although they do not have to much of things. It's not as bad as one might expect.

Their towns are modern and most living places not to bad. in fact I would mind owning so of these quaint little places with their thatched roofs. The farm are kind of built around a court or square and the home and barn and livestock with feed just go around and around and sometimes over lap. There's plenty of noise to lul one to asleep. Sheep. Pigs. chickens. horses. cattle. cats and dogs. and hay to sleep on. We get to use the

Appendix P (page 4 of 4)

barns once in a while and have used up a lot of these farmers hay. That's a cheap price to pay I think although some of them give us the eye. I'll told their glad to help along. One might learn to like it here if they never lived in the good old United States.

I'll have to sign of now and see how the guard is set up. Pleasant dreams and dear ones greetings if I don't get around to it. Greet the old man when you write. My greeting to every one

Love
Vernon

Appendix Q
State Agent's Special Report, Doris Norgren, Age 16
April 25, 1933

State Agent's Special Report

P.O. French River, Minn. Box 128 R.#1
Palmers, Minnesota, April 25, 1933

To the Superintendent of the State Public School,
Owatonna, Minnesota.

Dear Sir:

I hand you herewith my report of visit to and investigation of the home of Mrs. Betty Norgren

residing in Twp. / City of Palmers Sec.

County of St. Louis who has applied for a Doris Norgren about 16½ years of age.
General appearance of place small house, covered with tar paper but finished off nicely inside.
Comparison with others in vicinity about same
Land cultivated 5 acres   Help employed none
Size of house 4 rooms   Condition good
Furnishings fair   Books and Periodicals some also piano and organ
Number, sex and age of children at home grand son, John Norgren, 18 yrs. old
Treatment of own children
Members or attendants of Lutheran Church. How often occasionally Distance
Distance to school 5 miles by bus
Schooling promised thru 11th grade if she can get that far
Reputation in neighborhood

Further remarks Mrs. Norgren, paternal grandmother of Doris Norgren, has always been interested in Doris and anxious to have her. She has remarked many times that she hoped to live until Doris is 18 so that she can have her with her then. I asked her if she would care to take Doris now and she seemed delighted with the prospect, and says that as long as she lives Doris can live with her.

John Norgren, Doris' brother has lived with his grandmother for a number of years and says he would like to have Doris come so he could get out and get a job. As it is, he must stay near home so as to be with his grandmother nights so she won't be alone. He says Doris would have a good home there and plenty to eat.

They own 5 acres of land and have a fine garden in summer and chickens the year round and plenty of fish. They live on the highway between Two Harbors and Duluth and just the highway is between them and Lake Superior.

The grandmother has some insurance left from her husband and gets help from a married son in Duluth and relatives live just next place to them. All seem to help each other and they have no worry about being able to care for Doris.

The home was clean and comfortable. They have two rooms down and two upstairs. Doris would sleep in the grandmother's room in a bed by herself. Doris can attend school every day, in fact the grandmother

I recommend that the application be approved and that Doris Norgren be placed in this home, no money clause.

Appendix R
Letter from Dougal Norgren to Deward Norgren
September 19, 1931

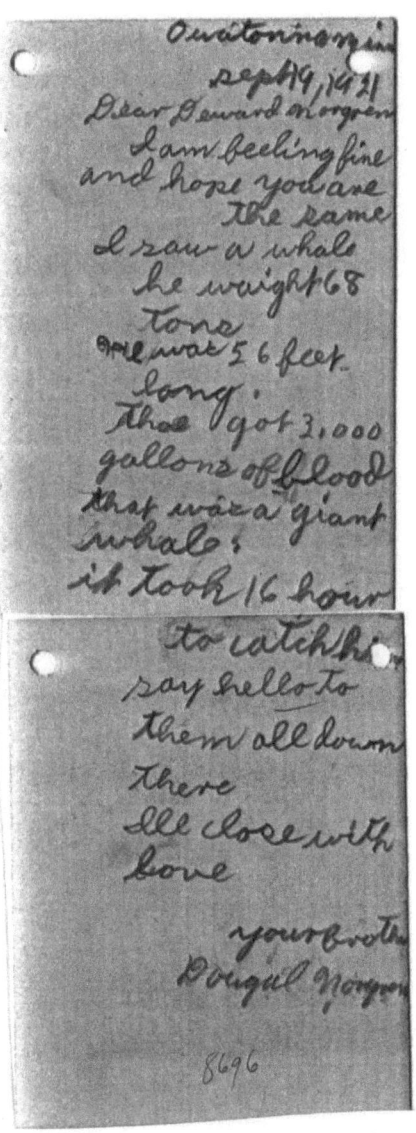

Appendix S
Hospital Records, Albert Norgren
1930-1933

DATE		Diagnosis	HOSPITAL	THROAT		
Entered	Discharged			Diag.	Antitoxin units A.M. P.M.	Date
6-14-30	7-28-30	Fracture rt. clavicle.				
9/19/30	10-8-30	Skin eruption				
10-8-30	10-9-30	Vomiting				
11-8-30	12-31-30	Skin eruption + U.R.				
2-7-31	3-16-31	" " " " "			?	
5-17-31	5-18-31	Indigestion				
1-8-32	1-18-32	Cat. jaundice				
1-7-33	1-11-33	U.R.				
5-18-33	6-5-33	Tonsillectomy				

CODE—Antitoxin units in thousands. B—Bronchitis. C P—Chicken Pox. D—Diphtheria. G M—German Measles. I—Impetigo. M—Measles
Mu—Mumps. O—Otitis. S F—Scarlet Fever. Ti—Tinea. T—Tonsilitis. W C—Whooping Cough.

Appendix T
Report Card, Albert Norgren, First Grade
1930-1931

Catherine Wright is a lifelong Minnesotan whose interest in memoir has been part of her healing journey. Cathy has always loved pushing boundaries and defying stereotypes. She began writing about her life when she joined the Lake Superior Writers Open Memoir group led by Mara Hart. Her passion for photography, art, and writing is grounded in the power of stories to help people learn about themselves and each other.